FINDING HOME IN THE PROMISED LAND

FINDING HOME IN THE PROMISED LAND

A PERSONAL HISTORY OF HOMELESSNESS AND SOCIAL EXILE

JANE HARRIS

J. Gordon Shillingford
PUBLISHING INC

*Finding Home in the Promised Land: A Personal History
of Homelessness and Social Exile*
First published 2015 by J. Gordon Shillingford Publishing Inc.
© 2015, Jane Harris

All rights reserved. No part of this book may be reproduced, stored in a retrieval system or transmitted in any form or by any means without written permission from J. Gordon Shillingford Publishing Inc., except for brief excerpts used in critical reviews, for any reason, by any means, without the permission of the publisher.

Cover and interior design by Relish New Brand Experience
Printed and bound in Canada on 100% post-consumer recycled paper

We acknowledge the financial support of the Manitoba Arts Council and The Canada Council for the Arts for our publishing program.

J. Gordon Shillingford Publishing
Box 86, RPO Corydon Avenue
Winnipeg, MB R3M 3S3

LIBRARY AND ARCHIVES CANADA CATALOGUING IN PUBLICATION

Harris, Jane, 1960-, author
    Finding home in the promised land : a personal history of homelessness and social exile / Jane Harris. -- 1st edition.

Includes bibliographical references and index.
ISBN 978-1-927922-11-8 (paperback)

    1. Harris, Jane, 1960-. 2. Homelessness--Canada. 3. Homeless persons--Canada--Biography. 4. Homeless women--Canada--Biography. I. Title.

HV4509.H37 2015   305.5'6920971   C2015-904859-1

ACKNOWLEDGEMENTS

This book could not have been written without the support of my publisher, Gordon Shillingford, who believed I had another book in me when I feared I had no chapters left. Thank you to the Writers' Trust of Canada and the Woodcock Fund for believing in the project, and to members of my writing community, Barb Howard, Gordon Tolton, Ann Douglas, and Denyse O'Leary. Thanks also to the Wellington County Museum for helping me find the wills, marriage records, and articles about nineteenth-century Canada that helped me bring Barbara's world back to life. Thanks also to the Alberta Federation of Labour and Basic Income Canada for helping me find resources on the Temporary Foreign Worker Program, Canada's so-called Labour Shortage, and how a Guaranteed Annual Income could work. Thank you to everyone who still fights to make Canada the land of opportunity. You all give me hope that we may yet reach the Promised Land.

TABLE OF CONTENTS

I. **The Promise on My Mantle** 9

II. **The Wilderness** 13
    Beginnings 13
    How Did It Come to This? 15
    The Meaning of Exile 19

III. **Fool's Paradise (Lost Again)** 37
    Just When You Think You Might Be Home 37
    Not a New Story 47

IV. **Driving Past the Poorhouse** 55
    When Promises Could Not Be Kept 55
    Our 21st-Century Poverty Industry 73

V. **Hacking Our Way out of the Wilderness** 119
    A Little Cup of Kindness (The Political) 120
    Scream Louder (The Personal) 125
    When What You Wish Isn't What They Want 130

VI. **Finding Home** 137

Bibliography 141
Endnotes 157
Index 185

I
THE PROMISE ON MY MANTLE

When I was six, I stood aghast at the sight of the Royal Canadian Legion Pipers, in their bearskin and kilts, marching down the street beside an overgrown park by the railway tracks in Drumheller, Alberta on Dominion Day. I was scared of soldiers, even old ones who had traded guns for shovels or cash registers, but the pipes mesmerized me. They sounded like a home I could not find.

On my mantle sits a picture of an Ontario farmer's widow dressed in mourning. The framed photocopy of a picture we thought was lost (until it popped up in a history book riddled with errors and written by strangers) contains a promise, not written in words, but in my great-great-grandmother's eyes.

Before World War I, putting on a widow's veil was a life transition that warranted a trip into the city to pose in front of a professional photographer. While all widows were expected to put on a black dress for at least one year of mourning, Barbara's pricey widow's weeds mark her as an untouchable lady of rank, a woman whose mourning was expected to be a life sentence.

Although she is about half the width of the diamond queen, Barbara Gilchrist does a fine impression of Queen Victoria, right down to the black veil and starched lace collar. The wide weighty sleeves piled over her arms, pressed black ruffles burying her thin chest, and hair-filled locket hanging from the metal mourning chain on her long neck—all signs of her position as a widow with a well-funded annuity and the big events of life behind her—don't quite hide the fact that she was once a hopeful highland lass, barefoot on the deck of a creaky wooden ship, watching home fade from view; or that she still has crops to bring in, teenagers[1] to launch, and hopes for them all.

She has high cheekbones, narrow brows, and drooping eyelids—like mine. But her beautiful wide eyes are filled with sad discomfort—probably at being corseted and pulled beneath the weight of her costly garb as much as over the loss of the second husband who lies buried beside his first wife.

Look a little closer. Her stare belies a hope outstretching her pinching corset. Canada has turned a penniless crofter's daughter into a lady who spends her days in a dress as unsuitable for labour as any the Queen wears.[2] The widow still dreams.

No doubt Barbara thought her own sacrifices were enough to ensure her children's children's grandchildren would never lose their home. Sadly, she was wrong. Though most of her descendants prosper, making a home in this Promised Land has never been an easy road. For some, Canada has been another place of hungry exile. And I have been among them.

I was caught in the poverty trap myself—twice. I fought my way out of that wilderness, but I still wear cuts inside my body and soul. More than that, my eyes can no longer look away from the carnage of human lives being devoured, on every street and in every town, by Canada's poverty industry.

Barbara's brood and their prosperous neighbours didn't ride past Wellington Country's poorhouse every day. It was about 20 kilometres away, on the road between Fergus and Guelph. Still, they passed it a few times a year when they took the big trip into Guelph.

Our generation is not much different. While thousands struggle to make a home in the place our ancestors insisted would be the 'promised land' of prosperity, we order lattes and dessert, oblivious to the fact that the cashier can't afford lunch. We drive gas-guzzlers past homeless shelters and food banks, not just in our cities, but also in our smallest towns, without a thought about our neighbours inside.

The taxes and charitable gifts the prosperous among us pay as tolls to avoid looking at the poor fix nothing. Instead, they fund a poverty industry that keeps the dispossessed in an exile thornier than any back bush squatter's camp.

It boils down to this. Our ancestors built poorhouses and soup kitchens to keep squatters from building shanties in their pastures and woodlots. We spend millions buttressing a multi-million dollar poverty industry that keeps the poor too busy cracking stones of futility and chopping their way out of the bureaucratic forest to help us bring in the harvest.

How did this nation of exiles come to accept first poorhouses, then soup kitchens, food banks, shelters, and a silent suffering class of working poor? How did charity, another word for love, become cold bureaucracy? *Finding Home in the Promised Land: A Personal History of Homelessness and Exile* is the fruit of my search for the answers to those questions. My great-great-grandmother Barbara's portrait opens the door into pre-Confederation Canada. My own story lights our journey through 21st-century Canada. I hope it helps us find our way home.

THE WILDERNESS

Maybe this is all my fault. *Notes, Winter 2013*

BEGINNINGS (PICTURING THE CENSUS OF 1852)[3]

Yeast smells. It fills my nostrils as I pound the sticky dough, flipping it over on the maplewood board Father fashioned into a cupboard. It is too hot in here. Fire, water, and the stench of boiling pork flesh burn my throat.

The windowless[4] kitchen is dark at noon. Smoke and ash from the wood stove suck away air and light. Sweat beads slide down Mother's forehead as she fights the boiling water pot. The cauldron spits and bubbles like a dragon as she stirs and strains to lift it from the heat. They say she was Sarah McAlister before she became the second wife of John Gilchrist.

I do not know if she misses home. But I do.

I am 12. My name is Barbara.[5] It means foreign woman, and I want to go home.

The sheep and the blight pushed us off the shore of home, and we became an island. First sailing, then tucked away in the woods. I was nine when the potatoes died on the field in the highlands, and we became a burden for the Laird. So, he sought tenants who did not complain. He put sheep on our land instead, urging us to start again along the seashore or in the towns. We did not want to farm kelp or make cloth in a factory, so we bought fares from the emigration agent. We climbed a rope ladder on to a ship waiting for us in the bay.[6]

Father was past 60 when we left home. We cried, but his eyes were dry as we hugged the last of our kin and left for the colonies.[7] He made a log shack to shelter us that summer we arrived in the Garafraxa district of Upper Canada. He fashioned it from the tall maples he cut down to make a space for us in the forest. He bent over the axe all day chopping away the blackness, opening a path for the wagon from our homestead out to the road to Fergus.[8]

Father's pay packet brought us food that first winter. It earned us a deposit on this land—our own farm that no landlord can take away—no sheep but our sheep, no cow but our own. The men built a school and a church. But that winter of 1849 was colder than the bitter winter winds and snow we'd known in the Highlands. Some days it was too cold and dark for the boys to go to the schoolhouse.[9,10,11] There was no chance of finishing chores in the light. The water froze and the fire would not start. We gasped for air as hacking croup shut our throats. The whiskey was gone by New Year's Day.

We drank it to soothe our sickness. We drank it to keep warm. We drank it when we made music. And we drank it in despair.

In the spring, we used our sharpest knife to slit the white shrivelled flesh of the winter potatoes. Once, twice, thrice, four times. We put each part deep into its grave, a hole dug out of the virgin earth.

It is John Gilchrist's sixty-third summer, and he labours for wages.[12] Sarah hunches her aching back and homesick heart over the potato hills and cabbage patch. Mary, Merin,[13] William and I pull weeds out of the ground. It is hot and we are thirsty. Only Samuel gurgles. Far from the blight in Scotland, we eat potatoes and meat.

HOW DID IT COME TO THIS?

It is January 2000, the beginning of a new century, and I am homeless in the country my ancestors thought would be flowing with milk and honey for their children's children's children's grandchildren.

How did it come to this?

Are these streams of icy water on my face all that's left of the ragged chunks of confetti snow that clumped together on my hat and hair as I walked through the storm? Or do only tears edge toward the muddy lake forming under my eyes, the delta of my confusion?

I blink, hoping my lids will dam the stream, at least for the second it takes my left hand to smear the stinging tide of mascara and water away from my eyes and onto my cheeks. My right remains fixed, wrapped around the heat of the mug that holds my coffee. The cream containers I picked up at the counter sit unopened.

Numbness from inside my head stares back at me from the burnt blackness inside my cup. I don't feel like drinking coffee. I don't even like coffee unless I cover up its taste with double cream and double sugar.

Bright lights and emptiness. I am the only customer in the place tonight. Only the desperate leave their houses to drink coffee in a blizzard.

Outside, it is a night to die in.

I have been watching an aboriginal man walk up Mayor Magrath Drive for the past half hour. He staggers on the ice in the parking lot about five feet in front me. He may do just that—die tonight—if no one forces him into a jail cell or on to a shelter mat. The green street light on the boulevard beams into the blinking parasitic Santa attached below its main bulb.

Underneath the beam, the aboriginal man's black hair dances wildly with the snow in the wind. His face is red with cold and alcohol. No boots. No scarf. No mitts. His black and red plaid wool jacket is barely visible against the snow clinging to its fibre.

I barely make out his eyes as he looks at me through the window, but I feel his fear. It is the same snowballing stabbing terror of being trapped outside tonight that is welling inside my own chest. Only the windowpane, a few loonies, and a friendly clerk keep me from fighting to stand on the same patch of ice he skids on.

"He shouldn't be out there tonight." I say the words without moving my eyes from the window.

The clerk shrugs over her tea towel. "I have seen him stagger in that parking lot at least half a dozen times this month. The street van will drive by pretty soon to pick him up. They will feed him a sandwich, and take him to the shelter."

A Blackfoot man freezing underneath a Christmas ornament does not puzzle her, but the clerk seems perplexed as she looks my way. I am full of 'pleases' and 'thank yous,' in my flowered blue dress, high boots, black wool coat, gold necklace and teeny pearl earrings. I sit in her coffee shop, twisting my ringless finger, pulling at my hair, scribbling in a notebook. Her stares make me wonder if my leather gloves and the fake designer purse on my table don't quite cover up the truth that I have as few places to go as the man flailing in the snow outside.

"Another cup?"

I nod. "Yes, thank you." I stand up to brush muffin crumbs away from the daisies on my dress. I carry my mug to the cashier.

Fluorescent lights glare down at the donuts and muffins scattered on waxed paper liners over the green and white checked shelves beside the cash register.

I am too tired to eat, but my table rent is due. I fumble in my purse for two toonies,[14] then point to a lonely bran muffin drying up under the light. "May I have one of those too?"

The clerk puts it on the plate. "No charge."

"But I can pay."

"No charge. You've paid enough tonight, I think."

I smile thank you and shame at how close she is to the truth. My stomach churns. I want to throw up, but I can't figure out what makes me sick. Is it the sugar in the donuts, the heat from the lights, or the puke orange and yellow walls meant to drive customers out after one coffee? Or is my gut churning from the black brew I have been drinking for the past four hours, trying to stay awake and stay inside? I can't guess. My head hurts.

Two heavyset Blackfoot men in green parkas and snowmobile boots get out of a white van with Mobile Urban Street Team (MUST)[15] written in black across its door. They pull their charge toward an open door and safety, despite his protests.

I pretend to write something urgent, brilliant, or both on a notepad. But it's not the stuff I should be writing. That won't get done tonight. I am killing time, delaying my entry into the frozen street, and decisions.

"May I get just one more refill?" This time I force the toonie toward the till.

I stall my departure until I can stall no more.

Street lamps and the full moon still light up the street, but the snow has stopped falling. I make out the maroon and silver paint on the cars in the parking lot. I glance up at the clock. It is half past six in the morning. I pull my coat off the chair and slide my fingers into my gloves.

"On your way?" asks the sleepy clerk as she wipes down the counter for the next shift. Her rag is a dirty grey from digging dirt out of counter corners all night.

"Yes. Thank you. For everything."

"Have a good day. Stay warm."

Grey morning rises as I walk past the park where my children played, past the school where I served celery sticks to hungry five-year-olds. I walk to the woman's shelter. I stand outside looking at the tower where women sleep in peace.

I walk up the ramp to ring the bell. And I stop.

Why didn't I go inside the shelter that morning? Well, I don't mean to talk in clichés, but it is complicated. The truth is I had knocked on that door a hundred times before, called, confided in the staff about my predicament, even volunteered—asked for help in a thousand other ways. And I came up empty every time.

They knew me well at that shelter; better as a volunteer and board member than as the plaintive anonymous voice calling for help in the night. Did any of the women I shared the boardroom table with suspect that I was as hopeless as the women bunked upstairs?

I pretended my way into homelessness. I left my first marriage, silent and convinced that there was no escape for me, that I would die under the bridge when my money ran out. Pretending that I could support myself after more than a dozen years as a full-time wife and mother, I did my best to hide the frightened little failure of a girl I was inside, covering up the awful truth with my mourning dress— long reddish dark brown hair, dyed black and tied back inside a clip, teetering high heels, and office dresses to cover my shameful inability to earn a living.[16]

By the time I stood outside that shelter door in January 2000, the deep shame I first knew as a little girl had grown into a conviction that no one should, or could, or would want to help me. It was as much a part of me as my blood and bones. The root of my self-loathing was my belief in the gospel that I must be inadequate to flounder in the land of promise my hard-working ancestors created for me.

THE MEANING OF EXILE

> Is exile in our blood? *Notes, Winter 2013–2014*

To paraphrase the *Canadian Oxford Dictionary*, exile is "expulsion, or the state of being expelled from one's native land or home, especially for political reasons"; or "a long absence from home, especially as constrained by circumstances"; or "exclusion from a group, accustomed place, etc."; or "a person expelled or long absent from his or her native land."[17]

In other words, exile can be chosen or forced. It can be spiritual, physical, political, social, or economic. Yet exile always comes with longing, and all exiles are driven to create 'home.' All poverty is exile, but not all exile is poverty.

Canada was built by exiles. Even Thomas D'Arcy McGee, a Father of Confederation, longed for his lost home. McGee's passion to create a new country in the wilderness could not erase his homesickness or the fear that he was forgotten in Ireland, the country he'd left behind:

> Am I remembered in Erin?
> I charge you, speak me true!
> Has my name a sound—a meaning,
> In the scenes my boyhood knew?
> Does the heart of the Mother ever
> Recall her exile's name?

> For to be forgot in Erin,
> And on earth, were all the same.
>
> Oh, Mother! Mother Erin!
> Many sons your age hath seen—
> Many gifted constant lovers
> Since your mantle first was green;
> Then how may I hope to cherish
> The dream that I could be
> In your crowded memory number'd
> With that palm-crowned company?
>
> Yet faint and far, my Mother!
> As the hope shines on my sight,
> I cannot choose but watch it
> Till my eyes have lost their light;
> For never among your brightest
> And never among your best,
> Was heart more true to Erin
> Than beats within my breast.[18]

In 1938, Scots-Canadian author Frederick Niven wrote that Scotland's migrants to Canada felt the same tug of home as they forged farms and villages out of the bush. According to Niven, "Scotland is a place in the sun and the rain, but more than that, it is a kingdom of the mind… the old love of it endures, whatever reason or necessity for living elsewhere."[19]

> "Pushing the bounds of knowledge and possibility comes with unavoidable risks." *Canadian former astronaut Christopher Hadfield, November 1, 2014*[20]

Visionaries are drawn to the wilderness. Perhaps that is why choosing exile on the frontier looms large in the Canadian psyche. It has inspired our poets, social reformers, industrialists, and our explorers. Among our national heroes is Sir John Franklin, who led three ships away from England in 1845, looking for the Northwest Passage. Franklin, the willing exile who gave up his life pushing through frozen wilderness, was the archetype of his generation.

As Franklin's crews wound their way through Canada's arctic waters in the 1840's, thousands of families, including my ancestors[21] John, Sarah and their children Barbara, Mary, Merin[22], and William,[23] poured into the wilderness of the Huron Tract.[24] Like Franklin's crew, they were intent on casting aside limitations.

While it's likely that the Gilchrists were Hebrideans who had hit hard times, many of their neighbours were from Perthshire. To keep their estates intact many Scottish landlords[25] raised rents and ran more sheep on their land. As early as 1818, the inhabitants of Perthshire were "reduced to such an extreme state of poverty that as to be unable to procure but one scanty meal per day" wrote a commentator of the day, John McDermaid.[26] Tough as life was, resettlement in Canada wasn't just an economic decision. Many families left secure lives in the Old Country because they preferred homesickness in Canada to life in a rapidly industrializing Britain.

Crofters and craftsmen opted to rise above their 'place' in the social order, rejecting the idea that they should abandon raising crops and their black cattle to fish, kelp, or dig canals so the Laird could run sheep in their old pastures. Even town-dwelling Scots who could send their sons to school and expected their daughters to marry successful tradesmen rushed to leave the old country. Some even risked losing everything by paying for their trips on credit. Their departures were festivals of music and dancing and well-wishes from neighbours who dreamed of saving up enough money to join them.

A few families could afford comfortable cabins, but most slept in the hold on wooden planks with porthole hatches battened down to keep the seawater from soaking them while they slept. Sometimes the squashed human bodies and cellar dampness made the place stink.

They left a bad enough climate for a worse one, accepting the perpetual homesickness as a fair exchange for a limitless future, believing it was better to suffer hardship and homesickness in the short term to become masters in their own houses forever. Once in Canada, those who couldn't afford to purchase farms right away put their efforts into getting land. They traded timber, built roads and worked as hired hands on homesteads in the Canadian bush. They slept in windowless shacks while they cleared new homesteads. They worked, saved and disciplined themselves to the top of the social heap. Where others would have given in to despair, the Scots thrived.

"Perhaps there is not race of people more adapted to the climate of North America than that of the Highlanders of Scotland. The habits, employment and customs of the Highlanders seem to fit him for the American forest, which he penetrates without feeling the gloom and melancholy experienced by those who have been brought up in towns and amidst the fertile fields of highly cultivated districts. Scottish emigrants are hardy, industrious, and cheerful—and experience has been proved that no people meet the first difficulties of setting wild lands with greater patience," declared Alexander MacKenzie.[27]

It wasn't long before the dark ships, shanties in the bush, and the cold first winters were forgotten by warm firesides in comfortable kitchens where settlers wrote letters to relatives back home about the good life they created in Canada.[28] Sometimes the kin were so impressed with those stories that whole Highland communities got on ships, intending to reunite their clans and recreate Scotland the way they always thought it should be in the Province of Canada. Highlanders became the strongest, most independent-minded, political and economic block in the Province. Even the poorest Scottish colonist refused to be treated as anything but an equal. In the words of an Aberdeen businessman who visited the colony, "the very lowest in Ontario…stand up briskly for equality, and in general insist on being admitted to the table with every master they serve."[29]

Still, even the most willing and successful Scots colonists missed home. Worse, they often experienced social exile—sometimes even found themselves subjects of angry sermons in the parish church—even before they boarded ships to the New World. While Britain's establishment endorsed Franklin's exploration as heroic expansion of empire and enterprise; they were largely myopic when confronted with the contribution made by upstart colonial Scots to British political and economic interests.

For decades, one of the few defenders of the emigrants, Lord Selkirk, was ridiculed by his peers for insisting that helping Scotland's poor establish towns, farms and businesses in British North America strengthened Britain's economic interests and fostered loyalty among British North Americans. The problem with Selkirk's position was that many Scots waiting at the dock to emigrate had money and trades to succeed in Scotland's changing economy. In her book *The Scottish Pioneers of Upper Canada, 1755–1855*, Lucille H. Campey quotes Lord Justice Clerk Thomas Miller complaining about prosperous farmers and mechanics leaving to attain "a better situation in America."[30] (Apparently, Miller was not unhappy when ships took away the poor.)

In 1802, a Perthshire clergyman named Alexander Irvine published *An Inquiry into the Causes and Effects of Emigration from the Highlands and Western Isles of Scotland with Observations on the means to be Employed for Preventing It*. He thought emptying out the countryside threatened the spiritual wellbeing of his flock and the financial viability of his parish. Despite this rejection by Scotland's officialdom—or maybe even in response to it—Canadian Scots held tightly to both culture and community once they got here.

Of course, they soon realized that they were not the only people in the country who'd been written off by folks they left behind. The United Empire Loyalists, who fled the Thirteen Colonies after the American Revolution, left behind businesses, farms, severed friendships, and family members who now called them traitors. Neither Crown land grants nor the letters UE[31] at the end of their name completely erased the memory of that past rejection.

The end of the Napoleonic Wars yielded another wave of social exiles to Canada—war veterans and their families. As the war machine shut down after the Battle of Waterloo, a severe depression hit Britain as thousands of soldiers were discharged from their military service. The prospect of newly unemployed soldiers threatening the stability of the Kingdom, by living rough and hungry on the streets of British cities, prompted the government to give veterans and their families land and free passage to British North America. In short, the veterans were thanked for their work and told that it was their patriotic duty to get out of the country because there was no future for them or their children in Britain. Taking up their grant of Crown land may have made economic sense, but discovering their country didn't want them after they risked their lives defending it, was a rejection that tested the heart of even the most loyal soldier.

One of the most tragic stories is that of the Gilchrists' neighbour, Isaac Woolner. A veteran of His Majesty's 43rd Regiment of Foot, Woolner brought his large family to Upper Canada in 1832. When he got there, the family rented a house in Hamilton that had been contaminated with cholera. The family became ill and his wife, Sarah,[32] died. Heart-broken Isaac placed some of his children in the care of local Mennonite families. Temporarily, he thought.

However, his son Jacob chose never to return to the family. The younger Woolner's decision was yet another disappointment for his father, but young Jacob did well in his new surroundings, eventually becoming a Mennonite bishop.

Isaac Woolner, a veteran of the Battle of Waterloo was no quitter. As he grieved his losses, he rebuilt his family and finances. He, his second wife Bridget Connor,[33] and their blended family farmed a large parcel of land in the Garafraxa District of Wellington County. The Connors and Woolners were close neighbours of my ancestors, the Gilchrists.

In 1863, my great-great-grandmother Barbara Gilchrist's younger sister, Sarah, married their neighbour Abraham Woolner, a child of Isaac Woolner and his second wife, Bridget Connor. While Sarah Gilchrist's husband is listed in official census, death and marriage records, he is sometimes missed in modern lists of Isaac's children. Modern historians may be confusing him with his deceased half-brother, also called Abraham.[34] Nevertheless, Abraham Woolner, Sarah[35] Gilchrist Woolner, and several of their children are buried in Trinity United Church Cemetery in Simcoe County, Ontario.[36]

Few groups understood exile as well as the Irish who fled starvation at home in the 1840's. In general, Protestant Irish—loyal to the Crown with family ties in both Scotland and England—were indistinguishable from the rest of Canada's Anglo-Irish/Scots establishment. Yet, the 1840's famine crossed the religious divide. Both Protestant and Catholic Irish starved when the Irish potato crop failed, and the nation rushed for refuge from hunger in Canada. Sadly, even the Irish who escaped the famine died in droves. Their experience contrasted starkly to that of the Scots during the same massive crop failure.

The worst year of the Irish Death was 1847. That year most of the 17,500 passengers who died of typhus or dysentery on ships en route or at the port of Quebec were Irish. Between 1847–1851, forty ships leaving the United Kingdom were wrecked. Most were Irish. The potato crop failure also accelerated Scottish migration to Canada, but Scottish ships were well provisioned and seaworthy. As Stephen E. De Vere writes, those who booked a fare in the hold of an Irish ship were squashed "like sardines in a tin, without light, without air, wallowing in filth."[37]

Even the Scots who stayed home weathered this massive crop failure better than did their Irish cousins. There were several reasons for this. In 1845 the British Parliament passed the Poor Law Amendment Act,[38] which made penny-pinching Scottish landlords responsible for the care of the poor on their estates. When the Highland Famine (1846–1856) threatened mass starvation, the landlords suddenly decided that Lord Selkirk had been right, and that the poor deserved the chance to seek new opportunities across the sea. They selected destinations for their surplus tenants.

Hungry or not, many Scots relished the opportunity to finally get their landlords to pay the fare to a country that promised more than mere survival. Some of them even faked poverty to get free passage. Between 1825 and 1830, 15,600 Scots sailed to British North America. Between 1831 and 1855, that number skyrocketed to 108,000.

Who Flourishes When Life Falls Apart?

Even among the poorest Scots, the lure of adventure played an equal role to the whip of destitution in convincing families to come to Canada. They thrived on the challenge, rising to the top of this country's political and economic establishment.

Their Irish cousins were not so lucky. In the 19th-century, it was often the Irish who lined up at soup kitchens or sought admission to Canadian poorhouses. Two thirds of people lining up at 19th-century soup kitchens in Toronto were Irish.

They weren't the only ones. England's disadvantaged sent to the colonies under the poor laws, without families close by, sometimes found themselves in situations as bad as or worse than the ones they'd left. Most had no experience with farming or rural life. They often wound up destitute in the wilderness. In the 1840's Alexander Galt convinced the Board of Directors of the British American Land Company that the surest way to save their failing colonization project was to sell the land to experienced Quebecois, Canadian, or American farmers who had proven ability to survive in the wilderness.[39]

Why? Were Scots, Napoleonic War veterans, French Canadians, and Americans really more suited than their neighbours for life in the new world? It sounds outlandish, but some research suggests that it may not be. Some would argue that the reason some people flourish in upheaval, while others flounder, lies in their genes.[40] Apparently, a variant of the gene DRDR, DRD4-7R, carried by about 20 percent of all humans, makes some of us more likely to take risks; explore new places, ideas, foods, and relationships; and enjoy adventures including moving to new places. Tom Cheshire, author of *The Explorer Gene: How Three Generations of One Family Went Higher, Deeper and Further Than Any Before*,[41] explores the possibility that those of us with settler ancestors have exile in our genes.

While the jury is still out on the explorer gene, there is mounting evidence to show that trauma can change our DNA, affecting life outcomes as the changes prepare the individual to live in a dangerous predatory world. Research conducted by Dr. Michael Meanie, Scientific Director at the Ludmer Centre for Neuroinformatics and Mental Health at the Douglas Mental Health University Institute at McGill University, suggests that, because maternal stress modifies the genes that regulate behaviour, stress response, and developing synapses in the hippocampus, a mother's stressful experiences can change an offspring's cognitive development and ability to weather stress.

In another study, a team at the University of Lethbridge found that daughters of stressed rats had shorter pregnancies than the daughters of those who had not been stressed. "One of the surprising findings of our study is that even if only the grandmother was stressed but not the mother, there were effects that persisted and even grew larger in the subsequent generations," explained University of Lethbridge neuroscientist Gerlinde Metz, the study's author, after her team's findings were published in published in BMC Medicine.[42]

A third study, published in Cell,[43] interpreted evidence gathered from animal studies and human famines to suggest that starvation may affect the health of the progeny of famished individuals. On a more positive note, the study claimed that starved worms lived longer.

If this mostly animal-based research truly transfers to real people living lives outside of laboratories, it may partly explain why some colonists shook off exile like a wet blanket and set about succeeding in Canada while their neighbours floundered in the wilderness.

Maybe the Scots were more suited to colonial life than many of their neighbours; maybe they were better at shaking off trauma and adapting to a new land. As the helping professionals put it; maybe they were more resilient. Or perhaps, the answer is even simpler.

> Instead of writing my book or looking for a job, I focus on bottle picking, selling my household items, and preparing for homelessness. My injury is made worse by the stress, so that I have no hope at all of lifting myself out of the situation. I am utterly alone and isolated. *Notes, Spring 2014*

When you don't have enough money, food, housing, work, or people to help you sort out the mess you're in, you also have too little time and energy to pull yourself out of that mess. The fear of not having enough lures you into worrying away your energy while you focus on schemes to stretch your money. Even worse, if you do get a windfall, your scarcity mindset sets you up to fritter that away, too. In *Scarcity: Why Having Too Little Means So Much*, Sendhil Mullainathan and Eldar Shafir write that the scarcity mindset shortens a struggling person's horizons, lowers IQ, and narrows perspective. Bad decisions follow.

Add isolation into the mix and not having enough becomes downright life threatening. If you are isolated, you will likely die sooner, poorer, and alone. A study published in the March 26, 2013 *Proceedings of the National Academy of Sciences* and re-capped in *Nature* found that socially isolated people are prone to illness and earlier death, even if the isolated person doesn't feel lonely. No one should be surprised by this study.[44]

Community was key to the success of colonists in Canada. The Scots were good at creating community. Highlanders sailed, set up towns, did business, and voted together. Of course, it wasn't just the Highlanders who stuck together. Lowland Scots weavers, forced out of their craft by industrialization and cheap Irish labour, created emigration societies that operated as co-operative friendly societies to help each other emigrate.[45] Their children attended school together. Even before arriving in Canada, the Lowland Scots were, by and large, better educated than other new arrivals. Since there were lending libraries in every significant town in Scotland, many Scots emigrants to Canada were already avid readers.

The advantages did not end when the Scots arrived in Canada. The Highland Society of Canada met every year, wearing Highland dress, on the anniversary of the Battle of Waterloo to raise money to help needy Highlanders living in Ontario. The Scots also retained their cultural integrity when they got to Canada. Presbyterians in Puslinch

Township, Wellington County held services in Gaelic and English until the late 19th century. Kingston had a Gaelic newspaper. This strong identity created a strong self-confidence that kept the Scots and their descendants from the worst effects of poverty.[46] Once arriving here, they quickly set up schools and libraries. In 1832, Scottish colonists set up their first public library in Canada in Dalhousie Township. The Scottish idea of using a property tax to fund local schools[47] remains a hallmark of Canadian school systems.

When life fell apart, the Scots emigrants stuck together. Other new arrivals to Canada, without family or community relationships, found themselves living in log cabins, giving birth on the street, or seeking a jail cell for a bed.[48]

Today it is still people without family support or community connections who fall through the social safety net into the streets, shelters, soup kitchens or jails. According to Citizens for Public Justice (CPJ),[49] immigrants, migrants, aboriginals, the disabled, rural people, single men,[50] single mothers,[51] children with young parents, and women are at higher risk of being poor. Additional risk factors for poverty include low income, high rents and utility bills, lack of food and clothing, unaffordable prescriptions and dental care, limited education, and intermittent work opportunities. Throw shame, family violence and mental illness into this witches' brew and you'll have an even tougher time keeping afloat financially. Still, none of these risk factors make it inevitable that you will fall through the cracks into social exile. Isolation does.

Isolation cuts you off from the opportunities, people and support that could stop your fall onto the street. Even before you fall off the grid, you can't afford to go for coffee, join a club, or socialize. You can't afford the bus fare to go the free movie at the public library. And you can't even begin to explain about your moods; why you are so afraid, anxious and overburdened.

As you fall into poverty, your isolation increases even more. Who wants to tell people there is no food in your house, or that you don't have a house anymore? "What is eating her?" they ask, never dreaming that you have nothing to eat. If you do trust someone enough to tell them your story, the relationship is never the same again.

Once people fall out of the middle class, society ramps up the isolation, blaming and labelling. In March, 2014, Creature Sightings, a Facebook page with over 200 members, sparked complaints and a police investigation. Members of the Calgary-based page took pictures of homeless people on streets of Calgary, posted them, and mocked the homeless online. The posters were upset and remorseless when the site was taken down. "What these people do isn't right,"[52] claimed one of the site's followers. He meant the homeless were to blame for showing up in public in the first place. The attitudes on Creature Sightings were barely more enlightened than those of 19th-century Ontario small-town residents who called out-of-work migrants wandering into their towns "pests" to be rid of with 'a well aimed dose of buckshot.'"[53]

Even today, some people are not satisfied with bullying social exiles. They beat them. In June 2014, a 47 year-old homeless aboriginal woman named Marlene Bird[54] was burned and cut outside the Margo Fournier Centre, a community centre in Prince Albert, Saskatchewan. She lost her legs and was permanently disabled. Ironically, her injuries finally got Bird a chance to come in from the cold. But why was she allowed to fall through the cracks? Where were the supports that could have ended her social exile before it started?

Sometimes we dress up our cruelty as civic pride necessary to keep our cities 'world class.' In *On the Street, How We Created the Homeless*, Barbara Murphy bares the meaning of 'world class city' as code for getting the poor out of valuable downtown real estate, then making sure they aren't seen by the wealthier folks who move in after them.

In May 2014, the people in charge of the East Village, a gentrification project in Calgary, Alberta, put benches and self-cleaning toilets on their fresh new Riverwalk paths along the Bow River. The paths are in one of the poorest parts of the city, just blocks from the Calgary drop-in centre. The bureaucrats at City Hall were horrified, and apparently surprised, when street people and shelter residents sat and slept on public benches and did drugs in $250,000 self-cleaning toilets. They locked the toilets and removed ten lounge benches.

In other cities, planners and real estate developers think 'mixed income housing' will be more palatable to middle and upper class home buyers if those projects include 'poor doors' to eliminate interaction between the poor and their richer neighbours.[55]

In June 2014, three more headlines dominated Canadian media in less than a week. In one, a music store owned by telecommunications giant Quebecor installed 'anti-homeless' spikes to prevent the poor from sitting on window sills or sleeping in doorways of a music store owned by media giant Quebecor. (When the story broke, the media company said the landlord was responsible for the spikes.[56]) Mayor Denis Coderre quickly condemned the spikes and ordered them removed as a safety hazard, a move that was entirely predictable since Montrealers[57] had borrowed the idea from London, UK. That city's mayor, Boris Johnson, condemned the spikes when they showed up in his city.

Calgary, too, was the scene of anti-homeless spike installations, reported *Metro News*.[58] "The rise in anti-homeless design has coincided with several laudable local anti-poverty efforts including the 10-Year Plan to End Homelessness and the city's poverty reduction strategy," wrote Jeremy Klaszus in Urban Compass Calgary, published in *Metro News*, July 7, 2014. Anti-homeless designs included spikes in doorways, curvy benches with dividers to prevent sleeping, and locked bathrooms. "If you were disturbed by the anti-homeless spikes in London, consider Calgary," suggested Klaszus.

The spike stories also sparked a regurgitation of media flurry about a June 2013 lawsuit launched after a park in Abbotsford, British Columbia was sprayed with chicken manure to prevent homeless people sleeping there.

Social exiles get it. Nobody wants them.

> I just don't see it tonight. I don't know how I am going to make ends meet. I am stuck. I can't see over the hill. *Notes, Spring 2014*

In the face of this inhumanity, you begin thinking that your isolation is nature's way of telling you that your survival isn't relevant to the herd. You know that you alone are responsible for your survival. So your body pumps adrenalin and cortisol as if you were facing a pack of wolves with only your own wits and a stick. You have no one to carry you when you fall. There is no rest. No wonder your health fails or you do not get better from your illness.

In Ontario alone, 230,000 adults contemplated suicide in 2014. Research linking suicide to social exile is convincing.[59] According to the Conference Board of Canada,[60] the social isolation that comes from poverty puts the poor at greater risk of suicide. In 2009, researchers from the University of Montreal connected material deprivation with increased risk of suicide in a paper titled, *Socio-economic inequalities in suicide attempts and suicide mortality in Quebec, Canada, 1990–2005*.[61] In the past year, several newspapers from the *National Post* in Canada to the *Daily Mail* in the UK have printed stories about the poor from India to Britain, choosing suicide over poverty.

It's no small wonder. Isolation, shame and unworthiness go to the heart of your being—you feel them in your chest. They won't go away—they defy counselling, preaching, loving and believing. They tear down what the brain would build up. Social isolation is the ultimate exile, and it puts you one step away from suicide.

Isolation makes it harder to bounce back. With no pension, savings, or stable job, one small setback puts you on the brink of homelessness, and social service agencies don't help much. As you wait for your number to come up in waiting rooms, it is obvious their departments are set up to make work easier for bureaucrats who don't grasp or care that human beings in crisis have unique stories and their needs are more urgent than application hoops, procedural circles or program mandates.

You give up on even making another call for help. Maybe it's easier to stretch or not to take your medicine than go begging for a subsidy, if you even know there is one available for you. You realize that getting help will take more energy than you have. You think about giving up who you are and everything you have ever dreamed of being. God help you if you can't find something left to hope for because hope is the only thing that will get you out of black despair long enough to keep you from jumping off the bridge. Social exile is the worst kind of exile.

How do I know this? At both my lowest points, in 2000 and 2014, I was convinced that there was no escape for me, no one cared, and that I would die penniless under the bridge. Crazy thinking? Perhaps, but I was convinced I was inadequate to survive, either married or on my own, and that there could be no end to my suffering but death, and every time I rallied to fight my exile, I fell back down into the failure, believing I was utterly alone, completely abandoned, and that it was all I deserved.

Did what I believe make it impossible for me to get help from social agencies, friends and family; secure a job; or end my social isolation? Probably, but the thing also worked in reverse.[62] My isolation made me invisible and even more vulnerable. I am only here because I refused to give up my last smidge of hope. With the help of two counsellors, I began asking questions about who I was; how I fell through the cracks in our social safety net twice; and why I keep getting up again.

The first time I fell into social exile, I only spent a couple of nights drinking coffee at the donut shop. After a couple of scary experiences with couch surfing and renting rooms in houses,[63] I found a room above a hotel I'd been afraid to walk past, even when I contested a political nomination using 'politics that invests in people' as my campaign slogan.[64]

Most days, despair and determination fought a war inside me. Eventually determination won. Within a few months, I was back writing business articles, while I built my own small business doing communication work, mostly for cottage-sized food processors. There was no private phone or Internet at the hotel, so I got a prepaid cell phone for business calls, put my work on disk, and sent emails from public access Internet. For a while, I bartered office space from a client who had bigger dreams than her wallet. That ended when we both realized her idea of one hour's work and mine were different ends of the universe.

But the biggest learning curve wasn't at my desk; it was on my street. I learned that what I believed about the poor was not true. They were not all addicted, crazy, lazy, criminal or immoral. Most wanted to work, worked for irregular pay, or were disabled. My neighbours inside the hotel were a community that did what they could to help each other. There were a few women, but mostly men lived there, made poor by disability, mental illness, or divorce. They stashed themselves away in grubby rooms above the bar.

I was surprised by what I saw 'good citizens' do to people on my street. One sunny afternoon, I watched two 'respectable' businessmen step over an unconscious aboriginal man lying on the sidewalk, without even bothering to check to see whether or not he had succumbed to a heart attack.

Another morning, on my way to grab a cheap coffee, I saw a man bleeding from his mouth. He stood dazed, just staring at the street outside the mall. I caught sight of a couple of clean-shaven, bright-eyed, twenty-something security guards—they looked like they might also be criminal justice students from the college—inside the mall doors. I asked them to call an ambulance for the man bleeding outside in front of the traffic lights. They laughed. "Is this a native by any chance?" The ugly attitude behind such innocent faces caught me by surprise.[65]

One winter afternoon, I noticed an aboriginal girl, she couldn't have been more than fourteen, shivering on the steps of a hotel with such a bad reputation that the people living in my hotel wouldn't go inside.[66] But there she sat, without mitts or boots or winter coat, just a block or so away from the youth emergency shelter. I asked her if she was OK. She seemed too afraid to answer. I went to do my errands, but I couldn't shake her image. So, I came back a few minutes later to give her my gloves. She was gone.

Another night a few weeks later, I was coming home from a meeting when I noticed another teenage girl. She was crying. She looked scared. She looked like she had never been downtown at night alone before. She caught sight of me. She called out, "Do you know where Woods Homes is?" I walked her to the shelter door and watched her go inside.

We talked as we walked. She'd had a fight with her mother and been thrown out of the house. She couldn't have been more than sixteen. She had no money. She had no place to go. It was 10:30 pm. It was dark. Once she was inside the shelter, I rushed to safety inside my room.

There were more teenagers in the neighbourhood. For about three weeks, a teenage boy, his even younger girlfriend, and their baby lived down the hall from me. I don't know how that infant slept. All the rooms were above the bar.[67]

Once a week, I'd chat with the maids as they changed my sheets. One afternoon, our conversation turned to the old man with the magnificent head of thick snow-white curls; the old man I would pass as he sat on the stairs overlooking the lobby every afternoon. They told me he had cut a growth out of his leg with a paring knife rather than go to the doctor's office.

Within a couple of years, I'd pulled what remained of my furniture from storage and into an apartment in a better part of town. When my clients were slow paying, I took call centre jobs to make rent. By 2002, it looked like I was a member of the middle class again, but I never shook the feeling that I didn't belong in the middle class. In June 2013, I realized I was right.

III

FOOL'S PARADISE (LOST AGAIN)

Why do we have so much trouble holding on to the gains we made? *Notes, Winter 2014*

JUST WHEN YOU THINK YOU MIGHT BE HOME

June 22, 2013. The Old Man River crested in Lethbridge. They called it the Alberta flood. Said it only came once in a 100 years. They lied. The floods come nearly every year now.

That afternoon, somebody smashed my head open as I lay prostrate on the floor of my bloody bedroom. The neighbours ignored my screams. The window was open. When I finally escaped, I stood bleeding on the street, alone, while they mowed their lawns and tinkered with their cars.

When you think you're finally home, it's terrifying to wake up in the wilderness. Your desperate screaming 'why' reaches back to rewrite the script. It tries to take you home to the safe arms of mother (were those arms ever safe?) or to a summer game of tag, or the first night with the lover who just tried to kill you, or to the sound of your baby's first breath—away from this graveyard you can't escape from. You ask 'why?' but the answer never comes because 'why' is not a question. It is a demand, a toddler's tantrum, a protest. You rage at fate, at truth, and at the God you kneel before every Sunday, trapped in a past full of 'why.'

When my second husband and I moved into our new (to us) bi-level beside the coulees, it looked like I was finally home. I was the wife of an apparently prosperous businessman, preparing to write my third book, freelancing and teaching writing on the side while living in a house and neighbourhood I loved. The truth was that we were already in the wilderness. And the truth was in the writing I didn't sell:

"Just her body lives. She has become a shell, a robot carrying out jobs, and distracted from understanding what might nourish her soul, even that it might need nourishment. In searching for evidence of her own value she became detached from her purpose: agnostic, unbelieving when it comes to her own worth and a nihilist in spirit if not in body."

"She is already a ghost, isn't she?" somebody in my critiquing circle said when I read my draft aloud. Indeed she was, and she was me; penning my desperation on scraps of paper, pretending to write fiction, acting like I had finally found home.

"I don't want to leave. I just want to be free," I wrote November 2012. I tucked that paper deep inside my desk. Everything about our life looked good on the outside, mostly because I kept my husband's ambulance trips to the hospital a secret. Our life was unravelling, faster than I could say 'ambulance' to the 911 operator every time my husband wound up unconscious in a prescription drug-induced stupor. I knew the load was too heavy, but I wasn't ready to give up on my vow or the person I had made it for.

When we married December 4, 2004, I knew all too well that my husband had demons in his past, but as he built a business and we built a life, I believed those were behind him. Looking back, his too frequent doctor appointments and afternoon sleepiness that began a couple of years into our marriage should have told me something was up.

Even so, he was far sicker than I could imagine; even as he told me he was putting his university degrees to work in a new job at a bank; even as he told me he was working that last week, even as he sent me strange texts that Wednesday morning about a security emergency at the bank and the security guard escorting him to the bus stop for his safety.[68]

We lived well above the flood plain, so there was no chance of us getting wet. But as the river was rising, my husband and I filled water bottles in case the torrent racing from the dam overwhelmed the water treatment plant again. The river crested in the middle of the night. The rain stopped. We were sleeping.

About 9:00 am the next morning, we awoke to the sun sneaking through the bay window and bouncing on the mirror. "Hey, let's check out the river," one of us said. Him? Me? Both of us? Doesn't matter. We were eager to see what the water had done to the valley. As I grabbed my orange sundress and flats, my husband pulled on his blue shirt and jeans. After leashing the dog and shutting the door, we headed across the park to the shale path along the coulees. Stretching our necks and squinting our eyes, we measured how close the muddy river was to surging over the traffic bridge.[69] Not close at all, we decided. The crestfallen river was already well down from its highpoint, still wetting the pillars. We went home. As the sun sucked up rainwater, I stopped to chat with a neighbour; then returned to the path barely noticing my husband's snide comment about how I wasting time talking to 'everybody.' As our house came into view, we chatted about eating lunch in front of the television. I headed to the kitchen to scrounge up dinner. He said he would check movie listings downstairs.

I was banging around in the pantry when I heard him calling me from below the stairs. "Hey, Janie, tell me when the coffee's ready so I can come up and get it. You shouldn't be running after me all the time." I thought he was being helpful.

For months after I was attacked, I cherished the delusion that his offer to get his own coffee was my husband's last noble instruction to me before he 'went away.' But let's be honest. The madness had already set in, and the monster downstairs was hiding vodka and pills inside the couch.

His attacks started about 11:30 am. In the first, he trashed my office, dropped my laptops on kitchen linoleum, smashed the walls, and tried to lock the dog, without her leash, and me, without my shoes, on the back deck. In the second, he threw his Blackberry at me, whipped the dog and me with my laptop cord, smashed both my computers with his fists, choked me, then turned the laptop cord into a bolas, cracking the power box against my skull, while I lay in child's pose, blood oozing from the back of my head down my neck and onto the floor. He kept saying, "I will make you homeless. You're gonna be homeless." He took thirty-one dollars from my purse. Then he snapped my neck until it cracked and I saw yellow dots. I thought I was dying, that no one would find me for a week. I said 'God' inside my mind. My energy moved to my feet. I knew what to do. I gave one kick and knocked him against the wall. I ran. I grabbed my phone. I ran again, down two flights of stairs without falling or letting the dog out into traffic. I felt the heat of the pavement on my bare feet. I can still feel it. I was going to take a bus to Emergency, but I decided I was too bloody to get on the bus. Should I ask for help at Tim's on the corner? No. They'd kick me out for bringing blood into a restaurant.[70]

I dialed 911 from the bus stop. The court records say that I called for help at 6:11 pm.

After I escaped, my attacker went to the liquor store, bought vodka, and came home to drink it in the bloody crime scene. It was about 6:30 p.m. The police were already there, taking pictures, pulling bloody sheets and pillowcases off my bed; asking me how I got out of the house. We heard him calling my name downstairs. "I don't want to see him," I said. "You don't have to," the constable standing beside me said. They went downstairs, took him to jail, charged him with six offences.[71]

Somebody called Victims Services. They dropped me off at the hospital and told me to take a cab home when ER released me. I nodded as they walked out the main entrance. I wanted to cry, but not in front of all these people. The clock on the wall said 8:30 pm. I pulled out my cell phone, emailed my parents.[72] They never got my message. The flood saw to that.

I texted my kids. My screen lit up.

"Doug hit me on the head with the laptop cord."

"What?"

"For real?"

"Intentionally?"

"Where are you?"

"ER at the CHR."

"I'll be right there."

"I'm on my way."

Evening turning to night, we sit in the waiting room, avoiding stares by acting 'normal.' My head pounding, I feel sick under the lights. I want to cry. The kids chat about work, university life, and their friends.

I don't know why I am so thirsty. I get up to get a cold drink, and blood streams from my skull, down my neck, on to my dress.

Hours later, they take us to the back, where we wait hours longer. A nurse stares at us through the curtain once or twice. About 1:00 a.m. an ER doctor walks through the curtain to stitch up my head. He glances at the bleeding whip mark swelling on my thigh, but he doesn't examine the lashes and bruises on my back, arms, legs, feet. He doesn't ask about the choking or the neck snapping. Neither did the nurses. My half-frozen scalp pinches as he weaves stitches into the back of my head. I get a tetanus shot and a lecture about domestic violence before I go home with instructions to get my family doctor to remove the stitches in a week.

I can't find my phone though I've just put it in my purse. Panic welling as it always does when I have forgotten where I put something.

> Have I really hurt myself this time? Put myself in danger one too many times? *Notes, Winter 2013/2014*

Within 48 hours, I see flashes of light inside my head. I feel scratching in my brain when I try to use a pen. I cannot think well enough to write more than a few words on my computer. I have trouble understanding voices on the telephone. My texts are spelled wrong. Sometimes I send them to the wrong person. I cannot remember where I put things or why I am in a room. I walk crooked. I feel like I am drunk. When I follow up with my doctor, he thinks I have a concussion. I expect to be 'all better' by September. I never do get 'all better.'

I feel betrayed. I know my neck and spinal injury, brain injury, and emotional trauma weren't just the fault of the drug addict who spent ninety days of weekends in jail for smashing my head in and trying to snap my neck. They were brought on by a system that did not listen to me when I begged it to stop prescribing my husband the narcotics he abused and to stop sending him home half-crazed.[73]

I spent years calling ambulances for my 'sick' husband. While he waited for trial, he volunteered to help the non-profit mission housing him with their annual walk to end homelessness. At the same time, he supported foreclosure of our matrimonial home and told Alberta Health Services to cut off my coverage.[74] I am not sure what happened to the $24,000 we released from his Life Investment Fund to pay down the mortgage. He was supposed to put enough on the mortgage to keep the wolves away for at least a year.[75] At his sentencing hearing, his 'support team' blamed me for what happened.[76]

> Every time I call, they ask if it is a domestic case. I feel dirty and ashamed and judged even if the clerk does not intend it to be so. *Notes, August 2014*

There was not a thing 'domestic' about what happened to me on flood day or the horror that followed it, but the file landed on the 'domestic' desk, along with a whole pile of 'common assault/he said/she said/what did she do to deserve it?' cases. It got shuffled between

Crown prosecutors for over a year before the accused cut a deal to plead guilty to assault with a weapon and mischief. The animal cruelty, two counts of forcible confinement, and common assault charges were dropped. For maiming me with little evidence of remorse, he got ninety days of weekends and two years probation, along with the court's permission to continue seeing his narcotics-prescribing doctor. The one who kept him stoned and whom the Alberta College of Physicians and Surgeons found to have made mistakes in his treatment.[77]

I read my Victim Impact Statement to a stranger; my husband no longer appeared to be in that body, no hint that he even recognized me when I looked at him. There was no remorse in his eyes when I read my statement, only drugged-up dullness. But as I saw him at his trial, still addicted, still confused, still desperate, still clinging to his 'support team,' my heart broke. He didn't earn my broken heart.

> I am running as fast as I can and I can't catch up. *Notes, Feb/March 2014*

I was heading toward homelessness. Worse, for the first time in my life, I couldn't pull myself out of the pickle I was in. Our friends appeared more concerned that my husband was facing jail than that I was a walking basket case facing homelessness.

I was in the pit of hell—even God didn't seem to call back.

My kids became my caregivers thirty years too soon. My daughter went to retrieve a bag for me the night I slept at her house after I was injured; she was confronted with the sight of her mother's blood smeared on the walls, carpet and bed. The next day, she and her boyfriend changed my locks and helped me clean up the blood. They paid the bus fare to get me to the neurologist in Calgary. Otherwise I could not have gone.[78]

"Did you just get into another guy's car, Mum?" My son gasped as we left the doctor's office. "Yes, please just take me home." A few months later, I was in Calgary at my cousin's house, spending the night there before I went for more tests at the Foothills Hospital. A call came in. I put the phone on speaker because I have trouble hearing voices coming through my cell phone unless it's on speaker. "Mum, I came over here to work on a paper and check on Chloe.[79] There's a flood. You left the water on in the bathroom. I didn't see it until it ran under the door and down the hall." My cousins knew what to do; after the June flood, they had cleaned up a waterlogged house in High River. They told my son to haul the carpet extractor out of the garage. So, he lugged the machine up two flights of stairs and began siphoning water from the bedroom carpet. He spent hours at it. No university paper got written that night. Even so, the sour stench took a month to leave my bedroom. It's a sad thing when a sandwich falls apart.

> Chloe is resting on the couch, beside me. She needs to be near me, follows me from room to room. I'm clearing clutter from my head with a pen. We go headlong into it. Where? I need to go back to office hours at my desk. *Notes, 17 February 2014*

I turned my house into a fortress to shut out the world from hurting me again. But the bill collectors, lawyers, realtors and gawkers got in, all intruding on my pain.

I slept on the bed I had been choked on, in the room where my blood splashed on the closet door and stained the carpet. I couldn't get the stains out. Even when I slept all afternoon, I was tired. No matter how long I slept, I was tired. The lawyers[80] and the bill collectors made me even more tired. So tired, I wanted to die.

I scrimped on my medicines for months, and hit a brick wall the first three times I walked into the Canada/Alberta Service Centre. The first two times, nobody had time to talk to me. The third time, they asked me what I wanted. I didn't know. That autumn, some Alberta mortgage holders were granted temporary flood amnesty.[81] Our mortgage company rushed to foreclosure.

I am sick, but I have to tell the story over and over again to bureaucrats, lawyers, doctors, nurses, clerks, friends, and family. How are you doing? How are you living? How are you paying your bills?

I have no answers to these questions, but they keep asking. Prying, shaming me with their questions and lectures about how I need to get on with my life; few offer to help me; they tell me to pick myself up by my bootstraps and 'get over it.' I flounder with a brain that will not work, bills I cannot pay, and memories that terrify me night and day.

I pick up papers off my office floor, but when I write, it is at the kitchen table or in front of the television. I turn my office into a pile of rubbish with the vacuum cleaner, ironing board, clothes, my weaving, the carpet cleaner, and papers piled in high unsorted stacks. Painfully, I revise the book proposal I started before I was hurt. By February I have a book contract, but I am not well enough to multi-task, juggle deadlines or conduct phone interviews. I cannot go back to writing feature articles, not yet, maybe never. Instead, I write a 650-word column for a content provider to keep the credits rolling in. It takes me all week to write those 650 words. I pretend I am OK. And the more I pretend that I can manage, the more I am trapped.

With my brain still not able to hold memories, and my speech slurring sometimes, I start looking for a part-time job. I get one, doing demos for a few hours a week. When my bank will not spot me a $100 overdraft to buy bus fare and work shoes, my daughter does it.

I should not be working in a mall. I panic when anyone walks up behind me. I turn white with horror when I hear loud noises in the warehouse. I slur my words four hours into the shift. At the end of the day, I do the 'drunk walk' home from the bus stop and feel like throwing up. Sometimes, I don't buy groceries so that I will have money to take the bus to work, and when the prepaid "Breeze"[82] card malfunctions, I panic.

> Tuesday April 8, 2014. The bus driver argues with me, tells me the bus meter can't be taking off too much money, but it is. I can't afford this. Three dollars isn't much to transit, but it is all I have to get to work with and I have no cheque until Friday.[83]

My symptoms get worse. There is a permanent dent in my head where the stitches were, and sometimes it feels like my skull is breaking apart. Sometimes I feel an electrical river running through my brain.

I quit the demo job in the middle of a PTSD meltdown. My doctor writes a note restricting me to part-time work under limited conditions. I realize I am not getting better. With no stable income and no income support, I am terrified that I will wind up homeless:

> It is 1:52 am and I have been sitting here for an hour waiting to see if my last scrap of holiday pay has been deposited to my account. I am riddled with anxiety, sitting here, going over and over my email, Facebook, and bank account. Back and forth I go between them. Hoping for what? Some magic? *Notes, May 2014*

That same week, another note:

> I stayed awake for much of the night before falling asleep and being wakened by a call from the process servers who needed to serve the papers for Doug's trial. Too little sleep, less than five hours and I was up and dressed in a more desperate state than before trying to figure it out, how I was going to stretch a week's worth of house money over three weeks of expenses and months of bills. Even the groceries I bought looked petrified. *Notes, May 2014*

Writing keeps me sane. I write my way from jumping off the bridge. I write until the panic subsides. When I have no money for food I write. When bureaucrats drive me to the brink of suicide, I write. I write, write, write on scraps of paper. I write on my phone. Five, ten minutes at time, until the pain comes. Sometimes, I write through the pain, until my brain stops working. The words flood over the triple dyke of depression, physical injuries, and twisted thinking that has me settled in the pit of lowered expectations. My counsellor tells me to keep writing because writing keeps me alive.[84]

I keep writing. I keep getting up again. Getting up again is in my genes.

NOT A NEW STORY

Barbara's First Wedding Day, Gilchrist Log House, Garafraxa District, Wellington County, Thursday, 10 October 1861

My new best dress,[85] blue taffeta with flounces and bows on the skirt, trimmed with more lace than I have ever sewn on a dress before, hangs from the door above my new travelling boots. My new bonnet lies on the trunk at the foot of my bed. I've filled the trunk with linens and blankets and all my clothes. I am travelling again.

This time I am happy to go, but my sisters breathe deeply beside me, lulling me to sleep again. I almost close my eyes, but I hear Mother in the kitchen firing up the stove. Why hasn't she called us? Pulling my head off the pillow I look outside. It's not quite light, but my brothers are almost finished their work. William chops wood, while Samuel walks toward the house with the first armful of fresh kindling. I kick the blankets off Mary and Sarah.[86] "Get up. They'll be here soon." I think I sound like Mother. But the girls grab back the blankets and pull them over their heads.

"We have to milk the cow." They pretend they don't hear. "We have to feed the chickens." They lie wrapped in their sheets like mummies in a tomb. "We have to help Mother get the food ready before we put our good clothes on." Silence. "Get up now or we won't be ready." The girls giggle under the sheets. At last, Mother calls from the kitchen. The mummies[87] unwrap themselves and jump out of bed.

Today is my wedding day.[88] I am marrying Michael Smith, a Church of England Englishman. I wonder what Father would think of that.[89]

Father lies covered beneath the grass. We could not afford a stone[90] for his name. And we still cram ourselves into the cabin he built for us. We have no farm, but Mother toils over the potato and cabbage patch. We sell our butter, milk, eggs, chicken, and pork in town. It keeps us alive. It keeps the boys in school. It keeps us together. We are not hungry. We are not cold. We have not done badly in this new land.

Barbara is twenty-one in 1861 when she marries Michael Smith, son of Thomas Smith and Mary Warner Smith, and begins her new life as a farmer's wife. Like his parents, Michael owns his own farm. This move is one small step up the social ladder for Barbara. She does not expect to have to struggle as her mother does.

Sarah has kept her five children and herself alive in rural Canada West since John Gilchrist died. When the enumerator makes his rounds in 1861, he finds the Gilchrists still in their log house on the same property they lived on when he came knocking in 1852. Sarah has even managed to keep the two youngest children, William and Samuel, in school.

How would a rural widow like Sarah Gilchrist make a living in colonial Canada? Widows sometimes earned a living from taking in sewing or other cottage industries. She may have had an income from selling land, perhaps to her neighbour, farmer/hotelier/land speculator Manasseh Leeson.[91] While it is not likely that John Gilchrist left his family an annuity, Sarah may have had relatives nearby to help her.[92] Some records show Sarah's maiden name as McAlister. So, perhaps the John McAlister who witnessed Barbara's wedding to Michael Smith was one of Sarah's relatives. Since Barbara and her sisters were not enrolled in school, they may have had jobs, perhaps as domestics at nearby Leeson's Inn or as hired girls on a neighbouring farm. It is even more likely that Sarah sold her butter, eggs, milk and meat.

The family almost certainly grew their own food. It was easy to raise small livestock, and grow potatoes, cabbages, fresh strawberries, raspberries, and apples.[93] A few butchered pigs and chickens, and a garden's worth of canned produce could feed a large family all winter.

In any case, Barbara knows how to scrounge a living, and how to cope with unexpected catastrophe by the time she marries Michael Smith at age 21. She probably never expects to have to do so. Michael Smith is part of a large extended family in the colony. His parents, Mary Warner Smith and Thomas Smith, bought their farm in Wellington County soon after arriving in the colony from Leicester, England[94] in the 1840s. Their mortgage was paid by 1860.[95]

As a Smith, Barbara has many relatives in the county. She is soon too busy rearing babies and milking cows to think much about what kin might remain alive in Scotland, or dream about the perilous voyage across the North Atlantic she took as a nine-year-old, or even to remember that cold first winter in the colony. By the time British North American colonies celebrate Confederation, July 1, 1867; the couple have three children. Barbara probably thinks she has surpassed the hungry exile of her youth.

As quickly as the potato crop failed when she was nine, her security vanishes. In September 1868, she is dressed in black, huddled with three preschoolers and a newborn at the front of a church filled with farmers and their wives. Michael's coffin sits in front of the altar. At 28, Barbara Smith puts on widow's mourning dress for the first time.

Michael has died without a will. She is responsible for paying off his debts from their assets. Worse, as the mother to four children under age seven, she isn't in the position to build a business selling milk and eggs, let alone to bring in the crops.

As she stands over a fresh grave, no doubt the neighbours whisper predictions phrased as questions. Will she put William, 2, Rebecca, 6, Sarah, 4, and newborn Mary[96] in the orphanage? Parcel them out with relatives? Perhaps, she'll work as a hired girl to keep herself from starving. Surely, her father-in-law, is 'talking out of his hat'[97] when he says he's going to bring the crop off the fields.

With his 80th birthday well behind him, Thomas Smith shocks the neighbours. He harnesses his horses to the plough to feed his son's widow and his grandchildren. Thomas Smith[98] brings in the crop for his late son's family.[99]

Thomas's help notwithstanding, not one of Barbara's choices looks good. They are made worse by the fact that, unlike her siblings and mother, Barbara cannot read.[100] It may be that leaving the Highlands at age nine pre-empted her entry into school, and, once in the colony, she never caught up. Maybe that she did not 'take' to school. But without 'reading and writing' she must earn her living on the land. If she loses the farm, and if her family cannot help her, she faces losing her children.

At the west end of the Garafraxa District,[101] a middle-aged farmer, William James Boyle, is hovering over his Canadian-born wife's deathbed. Maria Kennedy Boyle dies September 04, 1868. She is 34. The husband she leaves behind is one of the most ambitious men in the neighbourhood.

Boyle has worked his way up from farm hand to yeoman since arriving in the Garafaxa district at age twenty from what is today Northern Ireland. The son of Thomas Boyle, he was raised on a farm six miles from Enniskillin, Country Fermanagh. He arrived in the county as a teenager, worked as a farm hand for four years, and then bought his first farm. His name appears on mortgages as early as 1854. Chances are, Boyle's a potato famine refugee, but as a literate[102] United Methodist,[103] he fits well into the county's English/Anglo-Irish/Scots establishment.

The widower Boyle is fourteen years older than Barbara Gilchrist Smith.[104] He too, never thought he'd go hungry again, but when Maria dies, his future is blown apart. As he puts the soil over his wife's coffin, he's up to his neck in troubles, figuring out how to plant crops and look after three children. If he can't, he might have to split up Thomas, 11, Charles, 12 and Mary Jane, 8[105] between Maria's relatives or send all three to an orphanage. He needs a new wife, and soon.

By the time she puts her X on Michael's probate documents in May 1869, Barbara Gilchrist Smith is Mrs. William James Boyle, and she's brought her four children to live on the Boyle farm. Is the romance sparked by love or desperation? We'll never know. Nevertheless, their families stay intact, they keep their property, and they stay out of poverty. In fact, Barbara's younger brother William gets a job out of the deal. When the census taker stops by the Boyle place in 1871, he's living with the family, working on the farm. Five more babies come within a decade, Robert,[106] Samuel,[107] Adam,[108] Alfred[109] and Sophia.[110]

The family's home life becomes a waking nightmare one March afternoon in 1882 when a colt drags young Robert to death. The gory details of the boy's dying moments—how battered his body was, how bruises covered his body, how his head was smashed open, how he died in the farmyard—are printed in the Fergus papers.

They try to forget that afternoon in March. William buys more properties. Barbara manages. The family grows wealthy. But Samuel,[111] the son who was in the yard with Robert when the colt went wild, blames himself for accidentally frightening the horse that killed his brother. He grows up to marry the one girl in the county his mother objects to.[112] He drinks too much and fritters away every penny his parents give him.

> The death of Mr. William Boyle of Garafraxa, which took place on Saturday last, removed a well known and highly respected resident of that township. The deceased was born within six miles of the town of Enniskillin, in the County of Fermanagh, Ireland, on the 12th of June 1826, and consequently was 71 years of age to a day. He came out to Canada in 1846, and after working around as a farm hand for four years, he bought a bush lot on the 8th Concession of Garafraxa, where he continued to make his home for the remainder of his life. His career is an encouraging illustration of what care, industry and good management will do for a man in Canada. Although he may be said to have began his life with literally nothing but a stout heart and a willing hand, he has for many years past been in comfortable

circumstances. The homestead consists of 500 acres, and when this is added to the farms upon which he settled his three married sons, Charles, Thomas and Samuel, the whole foots up to 1000 acres of good land, well stocked and well equipped in every way. Mr. Boyle was a man of quiet habits who attended to his own affairs and left those of other people alone. He was an obliging neighbour, a genial acquaintance and prompt and reliable in all business matters. He never sought or consented to accept any public position, although often requested to stand as a candidate for the township council. He was not an extreme man in politics, but usually voted Conservative, and he was a respected member of the Congregational Church.[113] He was twice married, his first wife, Maria Kennedy, and his second wife, who survives him, being Barbara Smith (Gilchrist). There were two sons and one daughter of the first marriage—Charles, Thomas and Mrs. John McClelland—and Samuel, Adam, Alfred and Sophia by the second marriage. Up till last October or November, Mr. Boyle enjoyed steady health. About the time stated, however, he became unwell, and it was afterwards learned that he was a victim of that fatal disease, cancer of the stomach. He recently underwent an operation the Guelph hospital there being a possibility that it might extend his life a few years. But such was not the result, for he passed peacefully away on the 12th inst. The funeral on Monday afternoon was attended by an enormous concourse of people, about 200 vehicles being at it. The exceedingly large attendance was token of the esteem in which the deceased was held far and near, and of the widespread sympathy that goes out to the bereaved family. The funeral service was conducted by the Rev. Mr. Bolton, Congregational minister, who made a touching reference to the high personal worth and hopeful Christian experience of the deceased. *Fergus News Record*, 17 June 1897.

When he is diagnosed with stomach cancer in 1897, William makes a will that ensures his wife has an income and a home for the rest of her life. He knows that Barbara has been perilously close to pauperism at least twice (when her father died and when her first husband died) since the Gilchrists left Scotland for the colonies.[114] He makes sure it does not happen a third time.

William Boyle leaves Barbara an annuity, a horse, a cow,[115] all his personal possessions and the use of his half of the house. He orders their sons to pay her rent. The children will be well positioned to care for Barbara as she ages. He divides up his land between his sons and stepsons.[116] His daughters and stepdaughters get money.

Barbara dies, not in a log cabin, but in her daughter Sophia's house at #2 Church Street in Guelph.[117] The Talbots are a prominent Anglo-Irish family. Sophia's husband, Wilbert, is the nephew of Alberta Senator Peter Talbot.[118]

Truth be told, Barbara could have landed in a breadline in almost every decade of her life. Instead, she wound up with an annuity, rent, and an income of her own. Of course, she spent years milking cows, raising kids, and growing gardens, years when it wasn't clear whether or not she would wind up enjoying a comfortable old age. But it was community (family) that turned her life from constant struggle to comfort. She kept getting up again, but she didn't do it alone. During her lifetime, thousands of less resilient or socially isolated widows did go hungry, did see their families ripped apart, and did enter the poorhouse.[119]

IV
DRIVING PAST THE POOR HOUSE

Our ancestors survived famines, floods, fires, plagues, and wars that killed their neighbours. Perhaps that is why we have so little charity in our blood.

WHEN PROMISES COULD NOT BE KEPT

Poorhouse and Hospital

A committee, appointed by the county of Wellington, at its last session, for the purpose of considering the advisability of erecting a poor house and hospital in this country met at Dalby's hotel in Elora on Wednesday last. Six reeves were present, and considered the question in all its bearings, and unanimously agreed, that a suitable site for the erection of such a building could be found midway between the villages of Elora and Fergus. The reeves of the different municipalities will be corresponded with in order to ascertain the amount each municipality pays annually for the support of its poor, and other necessary information will be sought, all of which will be reported to the Wellington county council at its sitting in June next. *Fergus Lightning Express*, 15 March 1872, p. 2.[120]

It is 1877. William and Barbara Boyle are building a stone house with swastikas[121] and crosses carved above the doors and lacy wood shades over the windows for their growing blended brood. They are building an inheritance they hope will secure prosperity for their 'children, their heirs, and assigns forever.'[122]

As the tradesmen lay stone upon stone of the Boyle home, an even more imposing stone residence goes up about 20 kilometres away, on the road between Elora and Fergus. The Wellington County House of Refuge and Industry will shelter and provide work to the county's destitute while they learn how to be thrifty and industrious. This home for the poor will be a progressive retraining ground, a place where the hopeless learn to hope again.

Somehow, the words 'county poorhouse' still get carved above the entrance. Even its supporters aren't celebrating the county's need for a 'house of industry' a.k.a. 'poorhouse'; the fine stonework, crops, and gardens surrounding the poorhouse tell the world pauperism has built its own estate in their Promised Land.

No parents want their children to end up in the House of Industry and Refuge. So, William puts his name on as many mortgages as it takes to secure farms for the boys; he saves as much money as he needs to give Barbara and the girls inheritances.[123] He ensures no one in his household will ever walk up the poorhouse steps.[124]

Some folks don't think there is much need for a poor house in Wellington County, or anywhere else in this growing Dominion. Not with the West[125] opening up, the railway bringing trade from the Pacific and Prairies, and Toronto growing into a factory town.[126]

A century after my great-grandparents and some of their siblings packed up to catch a train to the North West, Wellington County's House of Industry and Refuge is still welcoming visitors. As Canada's oldest surviving poorhouse, it is a national historic site.[127] The Wellington County House of Industry stayed in the pauper salvaging business until after World War II when it became the Wellington County Home for the Aged.[128] In 1975 the old poorhouse, re-purposed once again, opened its front doors wider than ever before as the Wellington County Museum and Archives.

William and Barbara Boyle's[129] house still stands, too. But their descendants don't own it. When their son Alfred headed west in the 1930s, he sold it. Those people sold it, too. The family is long scattered; their descendants mostly strangers to each other. That old House of Industry and Refuge is home to the documents, clippings and pictures that are all that remain of my ancestors' lives in Wellington County.

It wasn't the first poorhouse in the province. The provincial capital, Toronto, built a House of Industry in the 1840s. But Wellington County was still ahead of the poorhouse building 'curve' in rural Ontario. Wellington's county's destitute had been housed in their sandstone mansion for almost a decade by the time the Ontario *Houses of Refuge Act* (1890) provided county councils with grants of up to $4,000 to buy 45 acres to build a local poorhouse on.[130] Eventually, Ontarians built poorhouses in every county.

When it opened its doors in 1882, the new poorhouse eliminated the need to stick homeless locals and drifters in jail overnight to keep them from freezing or begging; and it was light years more progressive than some pre-Confederation solutions.[131] By the 1880's no member of the Township council would dare propose following New Brunswick's pre-Confederation policy of getting paupers off the street by selling them into indentured labour at auction.

Poorhouses were a form of indoor relief, meaning that the poor lived inside them. Other forms of indoor relief included orphanages, homes for unwed mothers, and even prisons, if they were used to shelter the poor. In general, those most likely to receive indoor relief were widows, children, deserted wives, and the elderly.

Life in the Poorhouse

The poorhouse was a 'safe haven' for socially isolated poor people, including low-income seniors, the mentally ill, and homeless people; or as they phrased it in the 19th century, the 'destitute, feeble-minded and aged.' But you couldn't just show up, you had make the local politicians believe you were one of the 'deserving poor.'

In Wellington County, you had to convince the reeve and township council that you were a clean-living Christian with no way out of your hunger but a cot in one of the poorhouse dormitories. If they agreed, the reeve signed a commitment form, and personally led you up the massive stone steps into an entrance probably grander than any doorway you had ever entered before. If you were a step away from freezing or starving, entering the poorhouse was a little bit like going to heaven. The thick poorhouse walls insulated you from ridicule and derision. Better yet, you gained a job and a community of nearly 70 fellow inmates.[132] Maybe you worked in the garden, or on a building project. Maybe you milked the cow. Maybe you fed the animals you grew for meat. Maybe you cleaned the place. Maybe you sewed the uniforms that clothed yourself and others. Whatever you did, you didn't go hungry, and you weren't cold. You slept on a cot in the dormitory.[133]

You didn't have many personal possessions, maybe just a watch or brooch or framed picture you scavenged from your former life, the life before you lost everything, but every Christmas you got a little something new—a handkerchief, pipe, or an orange—things you probably had not received for a long time before you arrived at the poorhouse. If you were young enough, you may have received permission to leave the poor house at least once to try life on the outside as a domestic servant or agricultural worker. If that didn't work out, you came back. If you were violent or mentally ill, the staff locked you in one of the poorhouse jail cells. If you were sick, you were cared for in the poorhouse hospital. If you died, you were placed in the washhouse where they washed your clothes. They buried you in an unmarked grave on the poorhouse grounds.[134]

Because poorhouse residents grew their own food, did their own building construction, and sewed their clothes, the institution was an almost self-sustaining community in which men, women, and children were sheltered from the distain of their old neighbours and rebuilt their lives. The institution met a very important human need—other than just bread and bed. It restored each inmate's purpose — giving them a job, opportunity, and responsibility to contribute to their new community. Poorhouses had, at their heart, the truth that people want to matter, and that the work we do convinces us that we do matter.

Still, poorhouses often failed in their goal to rehabilitate the poor by teaching them skills and trades they needed to prosper outside the poorhouse community. The phrase 'cycle of poverty' had not been coined yet, but some inmates got mired in perpetual dependence. Some people, especially the younger inmates, eventually did leave the poorhouse for new lives. Many did not, including a few poorhouse children who never left 'home' long enough to make their own way as adults.

Inmates who surely could have found a paycheque if they had been allowed to leave built additions, renovated, and maintained the facility. Among those who never left were folks competent enough to tend livestock, look after thirty acres of crops, orchard, garden and a strawberry patch. Men strong enough to build a wing on the institution, women competent enough to sew their neighbours' uniforms, never again found employment outside. Some of the notable inmates who never left include Jimmy 'the giraffe' Allen, who operated the House of Industry and Refuge's limekiln, and Leonard Howson, a nine-year-old from Eramosa Township, who entered the house in 1877. At age 35, Howson drowned on the property searching for a lost fishhook.[135]

Sometimes, multiple generations wound up in the poorhouse. Among them was Julia Everson's family. Her mother, Mary Jane Everson, was pregnant when she entered the poorhouse 1889 with Julia, 7, and her brothers, Leonard, 5, and George, 3. Mary Jane's husband, Alfred, was sick, couldn't work and spent more than a year in Guelph General Hospital. Her baby, John, was born in the poorhouse. The family tried to return to their hometown, but Mary Ann and her children came back destitute. Eventually, Julia's brothers left the poorhouse for work as agricultural labourers. Even her mother re-established herself on the outside. Not Julia. When she was sent out to work, she couldn't adapt and returned. She remained at the poorhouse for the rest of her sixty-seven years, until she died in 1948. For a few years, she had grandparents nearby. Mary Ann's parents, George Hollingshead, 82, and his wife Ann, 80, admitted to the house in 1907 because of 'old age and destitution,' eventually died there.[136]

Those who criticized the poorhouse system for creating dependence had a point. Inmates traded their freedom and adult responsibilities for security, submission, and dependence. Except for the day the reeve walked them up those steps, inmates weren't allowed to enter the building through the front door and they needed permission to start a new life on their own.[137] They gave up their right to privacy and a personal life. Romance, normal family life, and sex were not permitted. Men and women, even married couples, were housed in separate dormitories. The dormitories were crammed in so tightly inmates had to walk over top of other beds to get to their assigned sleeping spot.

Still, 19th-century Houses of Industry in Canada were not the scary places we read about in Dickens novels. Notwithstanding their terrifying reputation, even 17th-century British poorhouses provided inmates with a better life than many of the poor who lived outside. That's one reason the resentful public struggling to make a life outside poorhouse walls dubbed poorhouses 'paupers palaces.'[138]

In 19th-century Canada, concerns that poorhouses were too posh were behind cries to have those seeking refuge do more than make beds and grow apples. To quell those concerns, able-bodied men seeking relief and shelter at Toronto's House of Industry were forced into hard labour cracking stone. These harsh measures prompted worker unrest and a backlash from the city's poor.[139]

Canada's 19th-Century Labour Shortage

It was difficult for overworked tradesmen, shopkeepers, farmers, and even many labourers to believe that anyone could not find work or land to farm in Canada. It was even harder for them to understand why people lining up at mission houses and breadlines, who said they could not afford a train ticket west, would not help them grow food. Instead, rural Canada looked to British orphans to fill agricultural jobs.

Young children and teenagers from Britain arrived by the thousands to fill job vacancies on Canadian farms. Most had no parents. Some were the children of industrial workers, usually widowers, who didn't have enough income to care for their children. A few home children had mothers in domestic service who could not keep their children with them while they served aristocrats in the great houses of Britain. By 1895, 100,000 kids had sailed as child immigrants to Canada. Two thirds were boys.[140]

Child immigrants came to Canada from church-run children's homes in Britain. By 1889, the Canadian Department of Agriculture had registered 50 agencies bringing children to Canada. They including non-profit organizations like the Church of England Waifs and Strays Society, Barnardo Homes (its founder Dr. Thomas Barnardo's motto was 'no destitute child ever denied admission'), and Fegan Homes of Southwark London. Roman Catholics had their own emigration movement, headed by Father Nugent, a Liverpudlian, who moved to London under sponsorship of Cardinal Henry Edward Manning. Catholic child emigration began in Canada under New Orpington Lodge, Ottawa, in 1895, and Miss Brennan's Home for Catholic Children, Montreal in 1897.[141]

Kids living in children's homes in Britain were often given a choice between learning a trade or working in the colonies. Since Canada was described to them as a land flowing with milk and honey, it's hardly surprising many children opted to spend weeks sleeping in the hull of a ship to get here.[142] Girls who emigrated to Canada took up domestic farm jobs as 'hired girls,' but boys came to learn farming skills that would prepare them to take out their own homestead as adults.

According to Phyllis Harrison, editor of *The Home Children*, the choice to go to Canada to work on a farm was a sound financial and personal one for many British children. Even living with a poorer Canadian farmer compared well to what the orphans experienced in Britain. Farm households were warm and dry. They produced their own clothing, sometimes even weaving the cloth. The family ate fresh meat, churned real butter, and grew fresh vegetables. In the happiest placements, young people attended community picnics, dances, sing-songs, as well as sleigh riding and snowshoeing parties.

Sadly, not every Canadian farmer was kind or fair to child immigrants. Perhaps, some forgot that the Home Child Movement's primary goal was helping children create better futures. In any case, penny-pinching attitudes from farmers who used child emigrants to cut their wage costs marred the Canadian experience for many home children. For example, a farmer who was paid $5 per month to house the kids turned the Home Child Movement into a wage-lowering, money-making scheme by keeping the child immigrant's wage at $4.00 per month. Sometimes, farmers' children went to school, while child immigrants milked cows, weeded gardens, and did field work. Some farmers reneged on wages or were so abusive that children simply left before they could get their wages.[143]

Sometimes, the kids were not the only targets of their employers' scarcity mentality. Some rural folk who took in home children had lost sight of anything but money and work. "I attended church, sang in the choir, and many times walked four miles there and back. As a youth I was aghast at these old farmers, putting 25 cents in the collection plate, and taking 10–15 cents in change. The minister lived on a mere pittance, and school teachers got $250 yearly," said one of the former home children who shared their stories in *The Home Children*.[144]

Despite harsh treatment, many home children grew up to build successful families and prosperous careers in Canada. But no matter how well they did, lingering homesickness for the land of their birth was complicated by feelings of rejection. As much as they loved the opportunities Canada gave them, they smarted at the memory of exploitation, and grieved their losses as child immigrants. This interviewee in *The Home Children* describes his life in exile: "I am now approaching 70 and over the hill as they say. Only one thing I am certain of—my background of life has given me a very insecure and restless nature. As I grew older there was always that question, in my mind. Why? For what reason did our family have to be broken up?"[145]

Whether they were treated as valued members of the family, or underpaid and exploited, child immigrants looked forward to the day when their indenture ended. They left to cut timber, work the railway or a factory assembly line, or to go west and claim a homestead. They turned their forced exile into chosen exile.

Public Meeting in Fergus

A public meeting to those favourable to the formation of a company to settle in the Nor'-West was held on Wednesday evening last. The attendance was large. On motion made and seconded, Mr. John Craig took the chair and J.M. Shaw acted as Secretary. The chairman stated the object of the meeting shortly and to the point and suggested that Mr. Vickers, the projector of the enterprise, should give his views on the matter in Question. Mr. V. read a number of letters from different persons all of whom expressed their readiness to accompany the Fergus young men to the far west.

After the reading of the communication referred to, Mr. Vickers said that it would be well to organize at once, create a general fund to settle in Saskatchewan if found suitable. Move by Mr. Kelly, seconded by Mr. Vickers that those favourable to the formation of a company with a view to settle in the Nor'-West or the Red River Territory signify their intention. No person having signified their intention, the meeting adjourned till Wednesday evening next at the same hour and place, when more definite information will be laid before the meeting. *Fergus Lightning Express*, 15 March 1872, p. 2.

As former child immigrants joined Ontario farm boys on the trains heading west, rural and middle-class Ontario balked at giving soup and bread to those who insisted on remaining unemployed in the province instead of taking their chances on the frontier.

Who can blame them? Arguments against heading to the frontier smacked of entitlement and racism. In 1880, unemployed workers in Ontario protested the fairness of anybody suggesting that mechanics in Canada's capital "leave the city" of Ottawa when they had contributed so much to "building it up... It was nonsense to ask residents of the city to go away west and live with Indians and half-breeds, and to work upon the railway in British Columbia, competing with Chinese cheap labour."[146] Forty years later, The Toronto Great War Veteran's Association was outraged by "Back to the Land"[147] suggestions that veterans "take employment mucking in the bush."[148]

By this time, some of Barbara and William's grandsons were themselves 'mucking in the bush' on homesteads in Alberta. They moved west to join other Ontarians who headed to the frontier to start again in communities throughout Alberta, Saskatchewan, and Manitoba between 1880 and 1920.[149] Just as their grandparents had done in Ontario, they quickly worked their way out of sod shacks into houses with gardens, prosperous farms, and vibrant commerce. As some of their own children headed to the frontier, rural tradesmen and farmers in Ontario feared they would to be taxed into the breadline providing for those who refused to 'muck in the bush'.[150] They feared their land of milk and honey would disappear underneath the sea of shiftless ne'er-do-wells living on public charity.

This 19th-century feud over the importance of expanding our frontiers to survive as a nation remains with us, not just as East/West alienation, but also in differing views between Canadian provinces about the role of government and how the poverty industry should be managed.

The Costs of Housing the Poor

Putting paupers in poorhouses, when the country was looking for people with gumption enough to open up the wilderness, was fraught with controversy even before Toronto's poorhouse opened in the 1840s. As the provincial capital, Toronto attracted both immigrants and fortune seekers. Many ill-prepared newcomers struggled to survive.

In 1857, Bishop Strachan theorized that Toronto, with its "central position has become a sort of reservoir, and a place of refuge to the indigent from all parts of the Province."[151]

By the time of Confederation, Toronto had its own constellation of missions, homes, and aid societies. In addition to dormitories for the permanent residents, Toronto's poorhouse had a casual ward that operated much like a modern-day homeless shelter where men were fumigated, bathed, and deloused before they hit the road again in the morning.[152] By the 1860s, Toronto had an Orphans' Home, Boys and Girls Homes, and a Female Aid Society, in addition to the House of Industry and Refuge.[153]

Many of those familiar with the poorhouse system in Britain believed it would bring the failures of the Old World to British North America. Among those most opposed to the poorhouse system was Lieutenant-Governor John Graves Simcoe. He had witnessed the failings of the poorhouse system in Britain. There, landowners were burdened with ever increasing 'poor taxes' while paupers remained trapped in perpetual dependence on handouts. When he arrived in Upper Canada in 1791, more than 100,000 British subjects (in England alone) lived in workhouses. He was appalled to discover that his predecessor had already got the ball rolling on plans to build a poorhouse in Toronto.[154]

Simcoe put the brakes on that plan, to the delight of both radicals and members of the Family Compact who opposed a poorhouse for completely opposite reasons. The radicals opposed anything that reminded them of the class system in Britain, while the Family Compact was afraid of being ploughed under by the cost.

The plan to build a poorhouse was resurrected by Sir Francis Bond Head, Lieutenant Governor of Upper Canada from January 1836 to July 1838. Bond Head wanted a poorhouse built at Toronto to care for the poor, sick and unemployed. Unlike its British counterparts, he thought York's poorhouse could be funded by donations. However, few in the colony believed there would be enough donations to fund the poorhouse. Many colonists still feared they would be snowed under with taxes to pay for the upkeep of the poor.

When the Toronto House of Industry finally opened in the late 1840's, its goal was "the total abolition of street begging, the putting down of wandering vagrants, and securing an asylum at the least possible expense for the industrious and distressed poor."[155] The legislation read:

> That the persons, who shall be liable to be sent into, employed and governed in the said House, to be erected in pursuance of this Act, are all Poor and Indigent Persons, who are incapable of supporting themselves; all persons able of body to work and without any means of maintaining themselves, who refuse or neglect so to do; all persons living a lewd dissolute vagrant life, or exercising no ordinary calling, or lawful business, sufficient to gain or procure an honest living; all such as spend their time and property in Public Houses, to the neglect of lawful calling... That all and every person committed to such House, if fit and able, shall be kept diligently employed in labour, during his or her continuance there; and in case the person so committed or continued shall be idle and not perform such reasonable task or labour as shall be assigned, or shall be stubborn, disobedient or disorderly, he, she or they, shall be punished according to the Rules and Regulations made or be made, for ruling, governing and punishing persons there committed. *The Statutes of the Province of Upper Canada* (Toronto 1837), pp. 80–82, reprinted in S.D. Clark, *The Social Development of Canada: An Introductory Study with Select Documents* (Toronto 1942), pp. 232–233.

Fears that costs of running the poorhouse would burden industrious Torontonians did not die away after the poorhouse was built. In the 1870's, John Langmuir, co-creator of the Ontario Charity Aid Act, voiced his fears that the growth of the poorhouse budget would lead to onerous poor taxes because "the principle that further Government aid to such establishments should depend upon the amount they obtain from the general public cannot be yielded."[156] An Ayrshire Scot, Langmuir also found the operation of Toronto's poorhouse too permissive and open to abuse. He wasn't the only one.

The Undeserving Poor

Nineteenth-century Canadians were fond of the scripture that said that the man who would not work should not eat. The editors of the *Toronto Evening Star* picked up the thread:

> 'Ye work not, neither shall ye eat', has, as dictum the sanction of the Holy Writ. Nothing can be more demoralizing than giving alms to men who are quite able to work, but very unwilling. At the instance of Aid, the management of the House of Industry, one of the most costly and important of the Toronto charities, obtained from the City Council a large quantity of stone, with the intention of having it broken by the 'casuals', who resort thither for out-door or indoor relief. The complaint of these people generally is that they can find no work to do, and are, therefore, forced to beg. The truth, as tested experiment is that very few of them are willing to work, while all are willing to depend on charity for their living. The discouraging result of the labour test in the House of Industry, so far from causing abandonment of the experiment, ought to impress on the City Council the absolute and urgent necessity of making a more general appreciation of it. ...While we have nothing but words of praise for the many excellent men and women who do so much to relieve distress, we have no toleration for that good natured shiftlessness which prompts soft-hearted and soft-headed people to add to the

demoralization of those who are already paupers in spirit. The best tonic for them is a strong daily dose of hard, manual labour, with a threat of starvation on the one hand, and the inducement of decent living on the other."[157]

In 1873, *The Toronto Globe* warned readers that drunkards, spendthrifts, and people who refused to work might drive them all into bankruptcy: "Poor law is a legislative machine for the manufacture of pauperism. It is true mercy to say that it would be better that a few individuals should die of starvation than a pauper class should be raised up with thousands devoted to crime and the victims of misery."[158]

Not surprisingly, those who chose frozen Canada instead of Scottish factories weren't inclined to become cogs in Toronto's fledgling industrial machine. Still, they had no patience with those too weak, stupid or unlucky to keep pulling up stakes until they landed in a place where they overcame poverty. They had even less patience with those who claimed life in Canada's West was too hard; especially those who went begging on the streets or those who refused to work in return for relief. The way they saw it, the new Dominion had more land and opportunities than people.

Many colonists survived on meagre incomes by raising livestock and growing their own food. Their gardens and fruit trees produced potatoes, cabbages, raspberries, strawberries, and apples. They got their meat, eggs, and milk from the cows, chickens, and pigs they kept in the yard. Even low-wage industrial labourers took control of their own futures by using their paycheques to buy cheap land on the outskirts of urban areas, like Toronto. They built their own shacks, and warded off hunger by growing gardens.

This was a country where even widows, like Sarah Gilchrist, could put food on the table. If widows earned cash selling milk, butter, eggs, or meat, and by taking in sewing, working in domestic service or as a hired girls; surely any able-bodied labourer with a bit of gumption could find a way to feed and shelter themselves, or move west to try their fortunes there.

People who believed Canada offered jobs to people willing to work, that gumption and discipline could pull people off breadlines, that vice led to poverty,[159] or that scammers lived among them weren't completely wrong. But that was only part of the story. The argument that moral weakness was the sole cause of pauperism didn't reflect the daily life in the province.

When Wellington County's poorhouse opened in 1882, Central Canada was running low on homesteads, and heading to Manitoba or the Northwest Territories to find a job was a new idea. Most migrants who came from the old country still squeezed themselves into central Canada, working on farms, in trades or in retail shops, or as domestic servants. There were a few factory jobs in Toronto, but Canada was still essentially rural.[160]

Still, the population in central Canada kept growing.[161] As more settlers arrived, so did the number of hungry, homeless people. Getting them out of public view became a matter of urgency. That was the situation in 1876 when Wellington County officials bought 50 acres of land between Fergus and Elora for a poorhouse. The poorhouse would also function as a self-sufficient industrial farm.

Deserving Poor

> *Desiderantes Meliorem Patriam*" (they desire a better country), Motto on Canada's Coat of Arms.[162]

A few winters before the Wellington County House of Industry and Refuge was built, controversy raged in the local newspaper. A partly paralyzed old man insisted on living in a hollowed-out log on a farmer's field, just outside Fergus. The Township Council debated what to do. Even if moral weakness had caused this man's poverty, duty precluded them from letting him freeze to death. Justice and providence demanded that they be their brother's or sister's keeper.[163]

People who wound up in the poorhouse were disconnected from family and land. New arrivals from Britain who did not have family in the province were especially at risk. Among them was a homeless woman named Mrs. Wellesley Knowles. She had only been in Canada six months, when she screamed for help as her baby was born on a street in Fergus. She and her newborn were admitted to the poorhouse September 23, 1884, to the delight of her older children. The authorities had taken them to the poorhouse a few weeks earlier, but they left Mrs. Knowles on the street, destitute, homeless, and heavily pregnant, until her child was born.[164]

Any number of misadventures could make a person destitute, including failure to get a job after arriving in Canada, crop failures, hunger, sickness, injuries, and old age. Nineteenth-century hunger and homelessness was rooted in the ever-changing, many-faced forms of family break-up and dysfunction that still puts people on the street today. Some people had mental breakdowns, others didn't have skills for farm life, and addiction followed others. Fevers, falls, and fights killed able-bodied young adults, leaving the aged without support. Husbands headed to American factories or jobs as trappers and farm hands in the Canadian Northwest, sometimes forgetting about the wives and children they left behind.

Even the staunchest Presbyterian farmer knew that an elderly man, too sick to work, or a homeless woman, abandoned by the husband as soon as he stepped on Canadian soil, giving birth on the street while schoolboys watched, did not create their own suffering. The charities, churches, and politicians called those who could not be solely to blame for their own poverty the 'deserving poor.' Still, they insisted that even the deserving poor needed to change their thinking.

When the shouts to build poorhouses in Canada began, it was the progressives calling. They agreed with those who opposed 'handouts' that 'pauperism' was no matter of chance; and that it was usually the fruit of immorality, irresponsibility and laziness. They also agreed that its only cure was hard work, pure living, and discipline. But they argued the 'deserving poor' could be productive if they were housed in a refuge and given work and moral instruction to help them unlearn the bad habits their misadventures in life had taught them.

Deserving poor might be lucky enough to find charity. But the town drunk and the shiftless man who refused to work for his dinner would be left to fend for themselves until they repented and gave up their vices.

Many Canadians preferred 'outdoor relief' to 'indoor relief,' housing the poor in jails, asylums, and houses of industry.[165] Outdoor relief included handouts of food or clothing to needy people living independently in the community. It reached more people at a lower cost. Toronto's House of Industry served more people through its outdoor relief programs—giving food and fuel to needy families—than through indoor relief. According to its first annual report, 46 persons received indoor relief while a whopping 857 received outdoor relief.

There were no county poorhouses west of Ontario, but western Canadians took the lead in providing outdoor relief. Winnipeg's All People's Mission, later known as the Margaret Scott Mission, became the blueprint for effective outdoor relief right across the country. Its founder, Margaret Scott, a beloved figure in the City of Winnipeg, brought food and clothing to the city's destitute with the help of her pony, Jo.

Winnipeggers called Scott "The Angel of Poverty Row," Winnipeg's Florence Nightingale, or "St. Margaret of Winnipeg."[166] Scott refused a salary, and relied instead on donations to fund her mission. Her zeal was sparked by the misery she found in the capital of what was then Canada's newest province.

A widow from Colborne, Ontario, she came to Winnipeg in 1886 to take a job with the Dominion Land Office. She quickly realized that far from being a boom-town filled with unlimited opportunities for all its new arrivals, Winnipeg was a frontier city with a poverty problem. Migrants flooded to the city from Britain and Eastern Europe faster than jobs were created for them. Sadly, many found only low pay, and irregular paycheques.

Moved to be part of the solution, Scott quit her job to become a full-time missionary to the urban poor. She offered medical care, training for district nurses, and brought food and clothing to the city's worst neighbourhoods. Scott spent her nights nursing female prisoners.[167]

Scott's relief work got into the nooks and crannies of the poorest neighbourhoods. She met paupers and near paupers in their homes, seeking out those who were too sick or frightened to reach out for help on their own.

Together with poorhouse system, outdoor relief initiatives like Margaret Scott's Mission, breadlines, and fuel distribution laid the groundwork for the modern poverty industry.

Outdoor relief thrives in 21st-century soup kitchens, food banks, and social assistance programs. Indoor relief thrives in newfangled versions of Houses of Industry—homeless shelters, women's shelters, and even seniors lodges. Both indoor and outdoor relief thrive in 21st-century Canada with surprisingly few changes since Scott travelled the streets of Winnipeg with her pony.

Sadly, the reasons people wind up at the bottom of the social heap haven't changed much either. Modern social exiles may never have escaped a famine, watched their children die of cholera, or been forced to sleep for weeks at the bottom of a sailing ship. They may never have found themselves abandoned on the frontier with no money, land or firewood, but trauma and exile are still at the heart of people falling through our social safety net into social exile.

Why has so little changed in 175 years? Can't we do better?

OUR 21ST-CENTURY POVERTY INDUSTRY

> Why is it that bureaucracy runs like a giant call centre? Stressed sick people can't keep making calls, running to appointments, waiting the whole day talking to the wrong people. *Notes, Winter 2013/2014*

We're a lot like the Victorians. We drive past the poor on our way to spend our paycheques, too. While some Victorians labelled the poor 'vermin,' some of us call them 'creatures.' Others pour gasoline on them. Worse, we continue to throw money at a broken 21st-century poverty industry when, with a little imagination, we might create our own Promised Land, a country that gives all our citizens a chance at the good life. Nobody ever intended it to be this way. We just fell into accepting diminished dreams.

Maybe tracing our path from that of our ancestors can help us figure out where we made a wrong turn. Maybe it will show us why social exile, trauma and poverty continue to dog us.

So, how do we compare with our Victorian ancestors?

We don't know our history

Canada's Liberals and New Democrats argue about whose party created our national health insurance program; but the historical record shows a Conservative prime minister from the prairies, John George

Diefenbaker, also championed both Canadian health care and Old Age pensions.

Our system of social programs, National Medicare (1968), Workers' Compensation, and Old Age pensions, was put into place because Canadians across the political spectrum supported them. Canadian Public Health Insurance was supported by 80% of the population. During the 1950's and 1960's Old Age pensions also enjoyed broad public support, despite protests from business owners that they would drag down profits.[168]

Even at the peak of the Cold War against Communism, most Canadians did not confuse American-style Free Market Ideology with Canadian Conservatism. American-style Republican thinking was left to the fringe and populist extremes of Canadian politics until the 1970's. Canada's Conservative visionaries, including Sir John A. Macdonald, John George Diefenbaker, and Sir Alexander Galt, believed in being our neighbour's keeper as strongly as they believed that 'he who will not work should not eat.' Canadians have struggled with these conflicting dogmas for three centuries.

Only in the mid-1970s did our fears, that supporting the poor would drown working folk under a flood of taxes, appear to declare victory over our culture's other mantra: that we must be our brother's and sister's keeper.

We're still confused

Recent history aside, Canadians continue to have conflicting views about social exile, self-reliance, and poverty. We cherish the idea that our ancestors, once poor, risked life and limb on the frontier to turn wilderness to prosperity. At the same time, we know they pulled together to do it, and that those who did not have strong communities—the clan, family, lodge, benevolent society, local church—were the ones to end up in the poorhouse no matter how hard they worked. We remain just as aware that our lives can be destroyed by catastrophe. We know it whether we are Conservative, Liberal, or Populist.[169]

We still believe the frontier flows with milk and honey

Many Victorians saw Canada as a place where famine survivors and orphans could hack a life from the wilderness, and where each generation could push beyond the limits of the last. First Canada West (Ontario), then Manitoba, the Northwest Territories (Alberta and Saskatchewan) and British Columbia beckoned the hopeful. Our vast frontier fuelled our belief that hard work could pull the unlucky out of their bondage to poverty.

Today, immigrants and easterners still arrive in western Canada eager to get in on a purportedly bustling economy. But sometimes the hope is misguided. The streets of Calgary, Edmonton, Saskatoon, Winnipeg, and Vancouver are filled with people who came looking for the Promised Land and couldn't find a job or a place to live they could afford. Worse, the person sleeping on the shelter mat next to them may have been born within sight of the Calgary skyline.

We still institutionalize the poor

While many of us are horrified at the thought of indenturing children or locking up the poor in institutions, we appear resigned to squeezing the poor into taxpayer-funded homeless shelters. The impetus toward putting the homeless in shelters gained steam in the 1970's, decades after post World-War II Canadians decided inside relief was antiquated and not a solution to the problems that brought the destitute to the poorhouse steps.[170] Worse, we accept increasing inequality. According to the Canadian Centre for Policy Alternatives, the .002 percent richest Canadians have as much wealth as the 11.4 percent poorest Canadians.[171]

We still believe old myths about the 'deserving poor,' that those who spiral down the social ladder are inherently lazy and morally lax. Citizens who ask for help at food banks must present picture ID[172] and tell their story of abuse, loss, injury, or victimization—probably for the umpteenth time—to a helper who decides whether or not they deserve food. The same goes for those looking for emergency help from provincial social service agencies, legal aid, or even women's shelters.

We're especially suspicious of non-Canadians. In 2014, the courts forced the Government of Canada to stop cuts to refugee claimants' health care. A July 2014, *Lethbridge Herald* poll showed 69 per cent of the readers answering the question supported government cuts to health benefits for refugees even though the Supreme Court ruled those cuts violated the Charter of Rights and Freedoms.[173]

The media loves to run stories about the alarming number of poor children in Canada. Why? Perhaps, it is easier to evoke compassion for innocent hungry children than it is to get anyone to help out a single adult who, according to many, should get a job, get fixed and get on with life. If single adults do get help, they live on as little as $581 per month.[174]

Why do we act as if it is acceptable for people without young children, people without picture ID, or even non-citizens to go without food, shelter, or medicine?

We still don't want to look at the poor

Nineteenth-century social engineers created poorhouses and resettlement plans to keep the beggars off the street without overburdening the prosperous with their care. Today, the poor remain largely invisible. From homeless spikes in Calgary entranceways to laws designed to get teenage window washers away from motorists, modern legislators keep their jobs by following voters' demands to get poor people out of view. The homeless are still social exiles in Canada.

Where the Social Exiles Hang Out

The gift shop I have to walk through to get to the tea room is filled too full of beads, scarves, jewellery, and trinkets that look expensive. They're not. I pick up one of the bracelets in the basket at the front to check the price tag—only 99 cents.

When I was in the 'mommie zone,' this building was a dark, decrepit second-hand baby furniture and maternity shop. It's still dark, its floors and walls still unpainted, but its new owners have the place dolled up like a street person after she's won the lottery.

I have met a friend for tea.

I cannot afford to be here, but she knows I am writing a book on homelessness, and she wants to tell me her story.

So, we sit at the table in front of window, looking out on to the street. We order scones with Devonshire cream. They bring us tea in tiny teapots. Mine is gunpowder green. Hers is herbal.

I sip as she tells me how a bullying boss and workplace intrigue sent her immune system into a permanent spiral; how her life as a young professional turned into the grimy grind of West Coast poverty; how she moved from a nice apartment to a scary tenement; from a job researching aboriginal land claims to permanent disability. How she fought nine years with an insurance company to get the disability benefits she thought she paid for. She mostly lost.

What was the only thing that stopped her falling straight to the street? Her family came to take her home.

As she ends her story, I pour the last drop of gunpowder green from my pot into my cup. Not sure what to say. I am happy for her, glad she has found home, honoured to hear her story, but I am also a little jealous.

I haven't seen my parents or any of my siblings since I was attacked. Maybe it's because they know I always get up again, maybe they think I am tougher than I am, maybe they are overwhelmed because this has been a spectacularly bad year for our family. Maybe it's all just too horrible to talk about. But a year later, most of my extended family doesn't know what happened in my house the day flood waters covered much of the province. It's a shameful secret. Whether they intend it or not, I've gotten the message: I am damaged. I am shameful. I am isolated. I am an exile. And that puts me at risk of becoming homeless.

The homeless, and those in danger of being homeless, are, for the most part, invisible. This has not changed much in 150 years. Nor has the fact that you become a social exile before you become homeless.

Many of Canada's social exiles have at least a tenuous grip on an apartment, rented room, a mobile home or house. They may appear to lead middle-class lives. But to hold on to what they have, they juggle rent, food, bills and transportation with the dark terror that the street is only 30 days—or a few missed shifts—away. They know that if they get hurt, fired, or the family breaks up, an eviction notice won't be far behind.[175]

There's no doubt that some factors increase the risk of social exile. People from aboriginal[176] communities have long-standing struggles to get employment and housing. They face a quadruple challenge: racial discrimination, rural poverty and lack of economic opportunity near their communities, bureaucratic red tape when they attempt to improve their own lives, and as newcomers to urban communities, they may struggle to establish community and business contacts.[177]

People with mental and physical disabilities must also fight to get on solid financial ground. According to Murphy, the mentally ill released from asylums after de-institutionalization increased homelessness by 50% in the late 20th century.[178] One reason for this: Governments who deinstitutionalized mental patients did not shift money to community care. Instead they used it as a means to cut costs.[179] Lack of access to training, support and jobs continue to leave the disabled out in the cold when it comes to escaping poverty in Canada.

Less than half of adults with disabilities have jobs.[180] Fewer still have political clout.[181] According to Mario Levesque, a political science professor at Mount Allison University in Sackville, New Brunswick the number of people with disabilities in politics is well below their ratio in the general population. He researched 2,084 recent Canadian local election campaigns. Twenty candidates had a disability, according to the survey respondents. That's 0.01 per cent, a far lower ratio than the 20% of Canadians who have disabilities.

Former Alberta MLA Kent Hehr, a quadriplegic himself, gives several reasons for the under-representation of disabled people at the political level—most come down to social exile. "There's a multitude of challenges. To be disabled in our society means you're going to be underemployed, have less access to money, less access to education, less access to the ability to take part in our society," Hehr told Aly Thompson of the Canadian Press in July 2014.

The stereotypical homeless person is male, addicted, mentally unstable, aboriginal, unemployed and cut off from his spouse, parents or children. As mentioned above, all of the above are risk factors for homelessness.

Still, many homeless social exiles defy the demographic profile. Most homeless people are not mentally ill (65%-80%).[182] Most are not drug addicts or alcoholics (66%).[183] Most are not aboriginal (58%).[184] The homeless, like all social exiles, come in both genders and many ethnicities. Many are parents or grandparents. Almost one third are women.[185] Many work.

Stereotypes about the social exiles not living on the streets also don't fit reality. According to Citizens for Public Justice, single working adults and single parents are most likely to be poor. Murphy writes in *On the Streets* that only one in seven families were poor, compared with an astounding one in three single adults.[186] Ironically, some of the poorest single parents, those who don't have full-time access to their children, still do not benefit from supports including public housing for families and recreation passes, meant to help low-income families stay together.[187]

The rural poor are among the most invisible social exiles, say the authors of the *Alberta Rural Homelessness Report,* released in June 2014. Jeanette Waegemakers Schiff, PhD, and Alina Turner, PhD[188] write that "homelessness in rural communities is primarily hidden." The rural homeless couch surf, "double up" on accommodation, sleep in sub-standard lodging, or even spend nights in the rough under the stars.

The poor come in all shapes, sizes, ages, genders, religions, lifestyles, origins and ethnicities. You can be poor, even if you were born in Canada as a member of the so-called dominant culture. Nevertheless, the poor always live at the margins of society. They are social exiles, and trauma trumps everything when it comes to pushing people into social exile.[189]

Trauma and Social Exile

In Garafraxa last Saturday evening Mr. Wm. Boyle's son Robert, a bright boy 12 years and 3 months age, went out to water the horses. It appears that he was leading a 2-year old colt. He used a tough line for halter, both ends being fasted to the colt's head and made a loop at the centre, into which he thrust his wrist. The colt was full of spirit, and jerking the boy off his feet dragged him first around the yard and afterward galloped through a large field, the helpless lad being dragged along the rough ground by the arm all the while. A younger brother in the barnyard at the time gave the alarm at the house with all possible speed, but when the colt was caught Robert's skull was found to be split open and he was otherwise bruised and most horribly. He died in the course of a few minutes and never spoke a word after the accident occurred. Mr. and Mrs. Boyle have the warm sympathies of their acquaintances, near and far. *Fergus News Record*, 20 April 1882, p. 2[190]

When I was seven or eight, I peeked inside Great-Granddad's shack on the farm where my mother was born. The table in front of the cabin window hid under old fur coats, books, and a pile of trash. Squeezing through the door, half blocked with trash, I conjured up a summer afternoon, decades before I was born. I imagined Great-Granddad sitting there, in an old Sunday suit, its folds hanging off his boney old body like drapes, his greasy white hair uncombed, dirt under his fingernails. I pictured a Brown Betty teapot, beside the brown stained cup half-full of milky tea, and a packet of pipe tobacco on the bare wood table. I imagined Samuel Boyle, the son of Barbara Gilchrist Boyle and William Boyle, almost seventy, chewing on his pipe, making a halo of smoke as he watched his own grandchildren, my mother still a blonde five-year-old wearing ankle socks, running toward him through the grass from the house, while his Swedish daughter-in-law pulled weeds from the garden, singing words he didn't understand, and his eldest son puttered with machinery, still trying to turn his hill of dry prairie dirt into the Promised Land.

The shack was a big comedown from the house Samuel James Boyle grew up in, but it wasn't the worse place he could have landed, considering he had made a career of bringing home shame instead of a paycheque. He'd seen worse days than this.

He told anyone who asked, including his grandchildren,[191] that it didn't bother him to have seen his brother dragged to death by a hysterical horse. And no one, living or dead, connected the day ten-year-old Sam Boyle watched his brother Robert dragged to death by a colt that he frightened into bolting, with Great-Granddad losing the farm his father left him, emptying his bank accounts, buying racehorses and whiskey, gambling the groceries away, and lighting fire to $100 bills.

Samuel, Mary Ann[192] and their kids wound up living off family charity and hand-me-downs, so the story goes, until they escaped to Alberta during World War I. Granddad, their oldest son, was the first to come to Alberta. As a teenager, he quit working on his uncle's farm, and went to chop trees in the Manitoulin Islands. Blind in one eye, the Canadian Expeditionary Force didn't want him in the trenches during World War I.[193] So, Norman Boyle headed west when he turned twenty[194] to claim his homestead, and to regain opportunities lost in Ontario, along with his father's inheritance.[195] Our family has been trying to get the 'big house' we lost in Ontario back for a century now.

Could Samuel's failure to hold on to his inheritance have anything to do with his belief that he was responsible for Robert's death? Did his shame set off a series of traumatic events that still makes it hard for some of his descendants to hold on to what they have? It's not as crazy as it sounds. Trauma can make you poor. Worse, when you're poor, you're exposed to even more traumatic experiences.

The *Adverse Childhood Experiences Study* links childhood trauma to risk factors for adult poverty, including alcoholism, depression, illicit drug use, ischemic heart disease (IHD), smoking, obesity, suicide attempts, unintended pregnancies and violence.[196] The link between homelessness and trauma is even more striking.[197] A study published in the *Open Health Service and Policy Journal* in 2009, found that:

> Individuals who have experienced chronic interpersonal trauma often have problems sustaining supportive relationships, such as difficulty trusting others or problems establishing clear boundaries and setting limits with others. This increases their vulnerability to re-traumatization, and interferes with the development of adequate social networks for support in times of crisis. Individuals with Complex PTSD may have impaired immune system functioning and may experience poor physical health. They often have difficulty maintaining attention and concentration and may have memory problems. Their belief systems about the world are also altered and they often feel unsafe…exposure to traumatic stress may increase people's vulnerability to becoming homeless in certain situations, and conversely, traumatic stress reactions may make it more difficult to cope with the stresses inherent in being homeless.[198]

The study concludes:

> Homeless service providers who lack a basic knowledge of trauma will not have a context for understanding trauma-based reactions… these behaviours may be explained in the context of common reactions to traumatic stress. … highlights the need for understanding trauma within homeless service settings.[199]

Worse still, there's evidence that trauma may enter our genes, and its effects can persist and grow stronger in subsequent generations, according to University of Lethbridge neuroscientist Gerlinde Metz.

In other words, discipline does not make trauma better. We lose our work ethic as we tumble into the pit of poverty, despair and hopelessness, not the other way around. As Will McLaughlin from Christians Against Poverty[200] told me when I interviewed him for a column I wrote in November 2013, "We assume people are (not responsible or spend too much money), but our most difficult cases are with us because of illness, job loss, or relationships have broken down… We can assume that we know the story, but these are sad and difficult stories. It's incredibly difficult for these people to get the help and support."

Tough Love[201] does not make trauma better. Yet, traumatized citizens, on the verge of social exile and homelessness, are put through a tough love inquisition or just plain mean-spiritedness anytime they ask for help from officialdom. They are re-victimized by bureaucrats paid to ask to protect the public purse rather than respect the traumatized person in front of them, every day, all day.

> This was a day from bureaucratic Hell, starting with the screaming match I had with a lady from the city—after paying nearly $300.00 in the last six weeks and giving up coffee and trips to church to pay down the debt. I haven't lost control like that in month, I could not stop screaming at the well-fed bureaucrat who told me it wasn't enough to keep my water on. I promised to come down there myself, hung up the phone, then calmed down long enough to realize venturing downtown would use up my last bus ticket and I would have to walk home after the security guards chucked me on to the street. I called the city clerk's office instead. A high honcho called back, nice but a little condescending. Nothing resolved, but he promised to get the supervisor I usually deal with to call back. Apparently, they weren't going to turn my water off after all. It turns out the city has taken to hanging these 'fake' yellow water cut off tags on customer's door knobs to 'remind' them to call the city. It sparked a panic attack in me, another meltdown. Just checked my utility bill. Bad idea. $1000.00. It's not been THAT cold. I am in full panic.
> *Notes, March 6, 2014*

You Can't Just Find a $10 Homestead Anymore

Exhibit 1: The Real Estate Market

A grey-haired woman—she looked about sixty—hobbled to the front of the courtroom. She leaned heavily on her cane as she moved. The mortgage company's realtor claimed that this disabled woman refused to answer her door and would not let potential buyers view her home.

The judge[202] was kind enough. He used his good father voice to threaten quicker eviction if she didn't do what the realtor wanted. It may have scared the woman into opening her door, but it didn't solve the obvious, most urgent, problem—that she had nowhere to go once the home was sold. *Notes, Master-in-Chambers, Court of Queen's Bench, Lethbridge, Alberta, May 2014*

Not only was this lady losing her home, she was losing any savings she had invested in it. Perhaps her house represented her whole retirement, what she cached away before she became disabled or some personal disaster made it impossible to pay her mortgage. While her foreclosure could open an opportunity for a young family looking for a smaller mortgage payment, there is a good chance a speculator will buy the house from the mortgage company at a bargain basement price.[203] If that is the case, her house will be painted, cleaned and resold at a profit by the new owner within the year. Flipping houses, buying a property then quickly reselling it for profit, is big business in Canada, but it may not be good for the economy.[204]

With housing out of reach for moderate-income Canadians, real estate industry speculators grow rich, pushing for bottomed-out prices on foreclosed homes and flipping houses for profit from desperate sellers to unsuspecting buyers. It's no surprise that the root cause of homelessness among those at the lower end of the economic spectrum is that "the low end of the housing market shrinking."[205]

Foreclosure speculators and real estate flippers not only keep real estate out of the hands of low-income earners, they put the entire housing market at risk of failing when the bubble explodes. Speculators contributed to the real estate market collapse in the United States in the early 2000's and continue to make housing unaffordable in Canada.[206]

Canadians spend more income on housing than almost any nation in the world, according to an October 2014 survey published in *The Globe and Mail*.[207] "On average, respondents said that they spend 43% of their income on housing costs (mortgage or rent plus utilities)—third globally to the Netherlands and Sweden—and have only 23% of income left over to save and invest—again, among the lowest rates in the world," says Black Rock Asset Management Canada, the firm that commissioned the study.[208] Those on the edge of homelessness spend closer to 70% on keeping a roof over their heads.[209]

One of the main culprits in our affordability crisis is downtown gentrification, which began in the late 20th century, and continues to push urban house prices out of reach for lower and middle income Canadians. Still, it's not just downtown real estate that is breaking budgets.

Gone are the days when you could put up a sod hut on your $10.00 homestead and grow enough cabbages and potatoes to eat all winter.[210] No municipality will let you live in a shack beside your cabbage patch on a half-acre at the edge of town, either. Maybe it's a good thing: 21st-century homes are certainly more comfortable than the old wooden houses our ancestors lived in. But we forgot to include everybody in our new housing blueprint. So, those who can't afford 'modern' housing are left out in the cold. We have built homeless shelters coast to coast, instead. Is that really progress?

Return of the Clearance Mentality

Affordable housing options, like mobile home parks, often prove unprofitable and unattractive for municipalities.

In May 2014, The City of Calgary announced it was closing Midfield Mobile Home Park in North East Calgary. When the last of the trailers leave the park in September 2017, 173 households will have lost the plot of land they park their homes on. With only $20,000 in compensation ($10,000 to move their homes, $10,000 compensation for the loss of their lots), and mobile home parks limiting their lots to new model homes, it's likely the most financially vulnerable among the residents will wind up in the rental market.[211]

When the announcement of the park closing hit the press, social agencies feared for the well-being of the mobile home owners.[212]

High real estate prices put Canadian families at risk for homelessness by increasing debt loads and monthly costs.

The third week of May 2014, the dog and I finally walked up to the step of a condo, just down the boulevard. The baby stroller was slung in the same spot over the railing on the front step; the running shoes peeking through the glass window on the lintel hadn't moved for a month. One white notice was pinned to the expensive-looking carved oak door. An identical one was taped to the patio door on the deck. I read the one on door: the mortgage company had moved in to take possession of everything on the property. I wondered what a mortgage company would want with a stroller and a pair of running shoes.

Jennifer Kismat, City Planner for the City of Toronto was interviewed by Tom Clark, Chief Political Correspondent for Global News during the summer of 2014. "One of the things that we did profoundly well a generation ago was to integrate newcomers, ensuring that newcomers within one generation could be a part of the middle class in Canada, and the risk to this today is housing affordability and ensuring that people can come into our communities, can come into the city, can live affordably, can get a foothold and can obtain post-secondary education and become a fully participating member of Canadian society," she told Clark. The interview was part of her pitch for a new urban agenda. Kismat wants Canadians to re-think the way we provide housing in our major cities to ensure we provide citizens with adequate economic opportunity and jobs.

The high cost of purchasing a home prompted the City of Calgary to go into the real estate market. According to the city-owned non-profit's website, "Attainable Homes Calgary spans the affordability gaps that stand between average, hardworking middle-income families and the homes they aspire to own." Attainable Homes Calgary Corporation is a non-profit organization owned by the City of Calgary that offers an affordable home ownership program for moderate-income Calgarians who qualify for a mortgage on a market value property. Attainable Homes Calgary gives these lucky buyers a head start on paying down their mortgage by gifting them a down payment.

Programs like Attainable Homes Calgary might help more people get into a home, but they do not tackle the obvious issue—overpriced housing. They don't help low-income Canadians gain independence from landlords, control their own futures. And that's a step back from the vision of Victorian Canada.

Some argue that land has always been big business in Canada. Of course that is true. In the colonial era, large tracts of British North America went to wealthy speculators.

The Gilchrists' log cabin was located in a part of Ontario that the London-based Canada Company helped open to settlement. Its founder, Scottish novelist John Galt, was a romantic visionary, committed to helping displaced Scottish crofters and unemployed Napoleonic War veterans purchase land. As the company's first superintendent, Galt offered these cash-strapped settlers small monthly payments on long-term mortgages and the chance to pay part of their mortgage with their labour. Unfortunately, the wealthy board of directors Galt put together to finance the Canada Company were more interested in making money than ensuring soldiers and crofters got homesteads. Galt soon found himself back in Scotland, disgraced, penniless, and unemployed.[213]

While the Canada Company, at least while John Galt was at the helm, offered long-term mortgages and low interest rates; some colonial landowners held on to large tracts of land hoping to make windfall profits. This made it difficult for new arrivals to find farms they could afford to purchase. In Lower Canada, these artificial land shortages led to the establishment of squatters' settlements, such as the Dalhousie settlement, established in 1820.

The Lieutenant Governor evicted the Dalhousie squatters. Still, it wasn't long until the land barons who refused to allow freeholders to purchase plots of land at an affordable price were unmasked as impediments to building the country. As famine, the rise of capitalism, and American threats to annex Canada pushed the British government to move more of its surplus population to British North America, speculators lost influence and the territory opened to allow greater numbers of aspiring freeholders to buy homesteads. By the 1840's, when my ancestors arrived in the district, Garafraxa had a real estate market more buoyant than that of many rural communities today. By then, new arrivals to the colony could purchase land from several sources, including local freeholders, estates of deceased colonists, and small-time speculators. The Canada Company was just one more seller in a competitive local market.

Renting Your Way out of Homelessness

> What's with the dim lighting in the hallways in apartment buildings and the worn ripped dirty carpets? *Notes, September 2014*

May 30th, 2014, I turned on the radio beside my bed to hear the morning news. Near the top of the newscast, I heard a story about renters being squeezed out of buildings they had lived in for years. Calgary-based Avenue Living had recently bought some buildings in Medicine Hat.[214] The company then boosted the rents by 50%, claiming that the extra money would pay for refurbishing the dowdy buildings. The tenants were not convinced. They began an online petition to ask the Province of Alberta to impose a rental cap. With the poor spending up to 70% of their incomes to keep a roof over their heads,[215] it is small wonder the local Public Housing Authority, Medicine Hat Housing, was expecting a deluge of newly displaced clients.

Avenue Living is a smallish player in the world of corporate rental companies. It owns apartment buildings across the prairies, including Brooks, Camrose, Edmonton, Lethbridge, Lloydminster, Medicine Hat, and Wetaskiwin in Alberta; Prince Albert, Regina, Saskatoon, Swift Current, Moose Jaw, and Yorkton, Saskatchewan; as well as Winnipeg, Manitoba. While this company is growing quickly, it is still a bit player in the world of corporate landlords.

The working poor live in fear of homelessness. They pray their housing costs won't rise and their incomes won't drop. The for-profit culture of corporate landlords puts them even further behind in the race to find and keep a secure roof over their heads. Even independent landlords hire professional management companies to ensure they get a quality customer—not a poor, under-employed, or addicted one. Housing is not a right; it is a commodity.

Social exiles are almost always barred from buildings managed by professional property managers, even if they come calling with cash in hand. Instead, the vulnerable go looking for a place to live where there won't be a credit check. They beg landlords and property managers not to ask too many questions. They dare not look to see if the furnace is inspected, whether a rented bedroom has a window, or if the smoke detectors work.

It is the last week of September 2014. The house is sold, finally. I am afraid that with no secure income and a year of financial disaster I will not find a place to live. I am afraid that I will lose my dog. I am afraid that I will have to live in a firetrap. Afraid that I am at the mercy of the rental industry, I go apartment hunting for the first time in twelve years. The first two inquiries I send out get prompt replies from Nigerian scammers phishing for social insurance and bank account numbers. Finally, I get a viewing.

As I walk up the driveway, where apples rot on the road, sinewy women in bargain-store short sets and running shoes come out into the sunlight. I hear dogs barking high in the tower. A golden retriever gets out of the elevator, led by a pale-faced, too thin woman who looks like she's still living a catastrophe.

I am terrified of being trapped in elevators, but I get inside this black hole with the building manager. The jerky trip up sends my head spinning. Still, it's not as bad as the stench of food and alcohol; nor as obnoxious as the drunk who hits on me when the door shuts on the way down. The apartment does not match the Kijiji ad. There are no huge closets. I don't see a storage room. The laminate floors are nice. The manager wants to impress me with the view, but I am terrified to walk toward the balcony door. She tells me she has another place like this one on the second floor.

She hands me some papers to sign. She wants me to give her a $1900 money order before she 'processes my application.' A cheque will not do as I could stop payment on it. She is vague about how I would get my money back if she refuses my application. When I ask about moving mid-month, she says that is fine, but she'll have to ask her supervisor if it's OK not to charge me for the two weeks the place is empty before I move in. As soon as I get myself into the light of day, I email her from the street. I tell her I am not coming back with the deposit. I tell her that I need to see more places. A few days later, a friend tells me that the dark tower I just escaped got its nickname, "Murder Manor," from a series of violent deaths inside it.

The second place has wood laminate flooring, a dishwasher, patio, and a park out front. My dog can move in, too. I give the landlords proof that I have money to pay the lease. They say I can have the place, if I pay the whole six months up front. It's no way to treat a brain-injured crime victim. The landlords don't care. With only a few weeks to clean out my house or lose my furniture, I take it anyway.

I get the keys and start to fill the kitchen. As soon as the Internet is on, the dog and I sleep there on an air mattress in the living room. The furniture comes mid-month. The movers overcharge me and leave a pile of boxes in my old living room. It takes me two more weeks to clean out the old house. I go back and forth every day with loads on the bus. I am afraid the first night I sleep on my bed again. I keep waiting for my husband to walk in the front door, and say 'hi Janie.' But he's never coming home again. I feel awful knowing that if he did show up, I'd call the cops on him. How did it come to this?

Is having a home a right? If the answer is yes, then perhaps we can no longer justify treating housing as just another commodity.

What's the alternative? Making housing a public service sounds like the perfect solution, but many public housing corporations have a track record of re-victimizing social exiles. They do it by treating tenants like 'undeserving poor' instead of customers.[216]

In the mid-20th century, federal politicians decided they could not let the poor live in their old run-down neighbourhoods. They passed the National Housing Act in the 1940s, thinking that clearing away slums would get poverty out of their cities. They squeezed the poor into projects like Regent Park in Toronto, a giant public housing ghetto that destroyed 13,000 privately owned houses (many rented by the poor) and displaced 20,000 people.[217] In the 1970s, the federal government's Neighbourhood Improvement Program (NIP) and Residential Rehabilitation Assistance Program (RRAP) ended the bulldozing of older neighbourhoods and started the gentrification craze in the cores of Canadian cities.[218] Gentrification made the old dowdy downtowns visually appealing and trendy. It resettled white-collar workers in spruced-up inner city communities.[219] And it continues unabated.

Residents of posh urban gentrification projects don't want the scruffy ne'er-do-wells from the shelter down the road hanging around their parks and cafés. God forbid that joggers or dog walkers should find a guy from the homeless shelter sitting on their favourite bench overlooking the Bow River, or using the self-cleaning toilets on their Riverwalk.[220]

Sheltering the Leftovers

> What is a shelter, but a modern-day workhouse, without the dignity of work? Don't we build them to relieve ourselves of the discomfort we feel looking at the poor and our guilt at seeing them frozen in the snow? *Notes, Fall 2014*

Shelters are the poorhouses of today—minus the work, self-sufficiency and safety. Old-style poorhouses shut their doors after World War II, along with homes for the mentally disabled, and massive mental hospitals. It was called de-institutionalization, and it was supposed help the vulnerable lead normal lives. Sometimes, it only made them homeless.

By the mid-1970's, institutionalizing was beginning its comeback. The move back toward re-institutionalizing social exiles began with non-profit agencies setting up shelters for abused women and their children. Today, Canada hosts a plethora of homeless shelters, youth shelters, women's shelters, and transitional housing projects.

We have task forces on homelessness in most Canadian cities. These circles of poverty-industry professionals hold countless conferences, conduct numerous studies, and meet for years on end looking for solutions. Sometimes, they even claim victory in the fight against poverty. Still, for all their effort, the homeless never disappear from our streets. Thousands of invisible social exiles couch surf in friends' living rooms or sleep in their cars because their jobs don't pay enough for them to rent a place of their own.

Usually made up of poverty-industry professionals, most of whom have little experience of social exile in their own lives, committees like Lethbridge, Alberta's Social Housing in Action (SHIA) keep tabs on the number of homeless people in Canadian municipalities.[221] In its *2013 Annual Homeless Count*, SHIA found 118 homeless individuals in this city of just over 90,000 people.[222] Even SHIA knows that its count just scratches the surface of the problem. The committee admits that its count can't reach the 80% of homeless citizens who couch surf with friends or family, or who cannot be found on the night of the annual census. The true number of homeless people in this smallish southern Alberta is probably closer to 500 people. The number of social exiles at risk of losing their homes dwarfs even this larger figure. And that's just one city in one Canadian province.

Well-run 'houses of industry' sheltered residents from shame; offering community and protecting inmates from the critical prying eyes of those who judged them outside. Once hungry, depressed, and frightened folk walked up those formidable steps into the protective doors of the poor house, they found companionship, dignity, work, and protection from nature's elements and public shaming.

Our 21st-century shelters and soup kitchens are filled with people without families or friends willing to help them. Instead they are mired in social exile, reminded daily that they are failures. Youth who wind up in homeless shelters may not get back on track for four or five years.[223] Homeless parents may never see their children.[224] Unlike those who hit hard times in the 19th and early 20th centuries, they have no dreams of a homestead out west, no possibility of a soldier's land grant, no chance to pay for land with their labour. They have nowhere else to go, and shelter life keeps them in exile.[225]

Instead of building shelters, maybe we should be building homes. Fortunately, Municipal Task Forces across Canada, including Alberta's seven Urban Housing Task Forces, are moving in this direction with a policy called Housing First. This policy places social exiles in homes instead of shelters. It is slow work, but Medicine Hat, Alberta began claiming victory at the end of 2014, predicting that 2015 would be the year it became the first Canadian city to eliminate homelessness. That's significant progress, but let's not get too excited. Housing First only targets the small percentage of social exiles who become public housing clients, or who wind up in shelters, jails, or on the street.[226] Most social exiles—especially the working poor—remain invisible.

Food Snobs and Food Banks

It is July 2014. The worker from the Brain Injury Rehabilitation Services has brought me to the Interfaith Food Bank. She thinks I need food more than rehabilitation. I am not sure I agree, but I come with her anyway.

Serious cash has gone into the refurbishing of this old fitness facility where people line up to get food for free. It is light and cool on a hot day. The tiny atrium is filled with flyers about services. I am startled to see shelves lined with expensive tomatoes on a vine, fresh dill, rhubarb, breads, water, pop. It's all stuff I never buy anymore. So much food.

She brings me over to a tall young immigrant woman behind the counter. We go into a small office to talk. Understanding people with accents is a problem for me since my scalp was split open by my attacker,[227] yet I connect with the food bank worker's kind eyes. I like her. She is respectful. For once, I do not feel stigmatized or judged by a poverty-industry worker. Maybe it is because the worker who brought me here is answering most of the questions.

The food-bank employee gives me a card as she tells me I can get a hamper once a month until September,[228] but I can also come in daily to get bread, pop and water, veggies, fruit, and pastries. (Of course, I won't be doing that. I don't have a car and I don't have time for daily trips because I am still trying to support myself.) We haul the hamper out to my helper's car. It has more food than I have purchased at one time in over a year. A paraphrase of a Bible verse I can't quite remember goes through my brain—something like 'eat and drink as much as you will for free.'

I come home with a whole case of sparkling water, cranberry and grapefruit juice. I have chocolates, and cookies, and ravioli, canned veggies, cold cereal, oatmeal, tomato paste, and ten pounds of potatoes. A few potatoes in the bag have gone off, so I pull them all out, wash them in cold water, leave them to dry in the sink. I throw out the two stinky ones. Five to ten dollars right there, sitting in my sink. But the hamper does not contain more than a smattering of protein. There is no fresh meat, no eggs, milk, cheese, yogurt or cooking oil. I would never buy so many cookies.[229] It is 10:22 am and I don't have to worry about what to eat today.

Today, Chloe and I do not have to go hunting for crab apples or return bottles for dinner. I sit down at my desk. I call the Community Arts Centre about organizing a fall workshop. I work on my column, and pull out my manuscript. In the afternoon, I take papers down to the courthouse. Yet, I can't escape the feeling that I am a bit tarnished.

The Down Side of the Food Bank System

Nowhere do the poor feel their exile more acutely than at the dinner table, where they can choose between feeding on scraps alone or going to an interview three bus transfers away to see if a poverty-industry staffer thinks they deserve food in their fridge.

Food Banks and the Dependence Myth was released in June 2014 by Food Banks Canada. This report confronts bias faced by Food Bank recipients from the general public, anti-poverty groups, and the food banks themselves. New clients have to prove who they are and tell the workers why they are going hungry before they get a hamper. The rationale for this scrutiny appears to be that food-bank staff think their clients are always on the verge of becoming hamper addicts. No wonder shame[230] stops 50 percent of Canada's hungry from stepping inside a food bank.

The underlying belief behind policies designed to prevent 'cheating' by food-bank recipients seems to be that the shame of not being able to afford to feed yourself won't keep handout addicts from showing up at the food bank. Nor will being labelled a failure by friends and family. And that getting a loaf of five-day-old bread more than compensates for being labelled 'marginalized' by 'helping' professionals. The poverty industry's obsession with making sure the only 'deserving poor' get free food hampers is even stranger if you consider that much of the food given out at food banks was headed to the garbage bin anyway. Frankly, some of what lands on food-bank shelves belongs in the trash heap, not in a poor person's fridge.

While most of my groceries from the food bank were great, some items were well past their expiry date. I opened one package of pita only to find that every pita in the bag was freckled white and blue with mould. A little mould never hurt anyone, did it? And beggars can't be choosers. This item could have easily been frozen before expiry instead of being left to go bad on a shelf.

Like homeless shelters, food banks are not a viable long-term solution to hunger in Canada. They are set up to ensure that many of the working poor cannot access them. For one thing, large cardboard hamper boxes are suited to clients with cars, not those walking because they are too poor to afford bus fare. Clients also have to show up during the day when many of the working poor are earning scanty wages to pay rent.

Still, people who get past the gatekeepers at the food bank are fortunate because many social exiles still go hungry in the Promised Land.

Plenty of self-employed workers and low wage earners would never dream of stepping inside a food bank, and it's not just shame that blocks the door. Unless they are between jobs or recovering from an injury, low wage earners do not have time to pick up fresh veggies and fruit every day. If they work in service industries, their job might include throwing meat and milk into the incinerator.

Then there is geography. Food banks do not begin to solve the problem of hunger in rural communities and northern Canada. In Canada's North, it costs $20,000 annually to feed a family of four. Seventy two percent of Inuit households in Nunavut[231] report not having enough food. Canada's Auditor General, Michael Ferguson, noted more problems as tabled his Fall 2014 Report:

> Food costs are significantly higher in the North. It costs on average twice as much to feed a household in Nunavut as it does elsewhere in Canada. One of the problems we found is that the Nutrition North Program does not identify eligible communities on the basis of need. For example, there are two communities in Northern Ontario that are about 20 kilometres apart and are similarly isolated. One is eligible for a full subsidy of $1.60 per kilogram of food, while the other is eligible only for a partial subsidy of 5 cents per kilogram.
>
> We also found that Aboriginal Affairs and Northern Development Canada has not done the work necessary to verify that northern retailers are passing on to consumers the full government subsidy on eligible foods. If the Department was able to verify that this was the case, some of the public skepticism surrounding the Nutrition North Program could be lessened. This would benefit the

Department, northern retailers and the residents of Canada's remote northern communities.[232]

In other words, federal support for northern residents is not applied equally across communities, and retailers may be pocketing the money instead of passing the federal subsidy on to hungry northerners.

Each month, in 2014, approximately 841,191 Canadians got groceries from a food bank. Twelve percent of those people had jobs. Another five percent were between jobs and receiving EI.[233] These figures don't include hungry Canadians who can't get to a food bank or are too ashamed to go. Surely, we can do better.

Remembering What Works

> Spoiled Albertans threw food on the floor and in garbage cans, they sneered at porridge samples and simple food. I wondered how many of these brats had ancestors who survived the potato crop failure in Scotland and Ireland. More than a handful, I suspect. Meals on ships carrying those exiles across the Atlantic consisted of beef, bread, biscuit, oatmeal, molasses and water. It was better than what they got at home. And we turn our noses up at oatmeal and mashed potatoes? *Observations I made doing food demos, Notes, Spring 2014*

Some food activists try to make fundamental changes to the way we distribute food in Canada. Nick Saul[234] left Toronto's The Stop Community Food Centre[235] to start a national network of food centres called Community Food Centres Canada (CFCC).[236] CFCC believes that solutions lie not in handing out hampers to the 'deserving poor,' but in returning to doing the very thing that kept colonists alive those first hungry winters in British North America: building community. "At CFCC, our goal is to take upstream action on the issues facing low-income communities. That means creating effective, replicable programs that promote health and community. It also means empowering people to engage in the issues that affect their lives, like speaking out about better income supports and more affordable housing," wrote Saul in CFCC's December 29, 2014 newsletter.[237]

Community Food Centres Canada provides resources and helps partner organizations establish local Community Food Centres where citizens across Canada can "grow, cook, share, and advocate for good food." In 2014, the CFCC launched a new Community Food Centre in Toronto's Regent Park neighbourhood, and began two more projects. By early 2015, the organization had already partnered with 37 organizations across the country "to support them to offer dignified and respectful food programs in their communities."[238]

Community gardens and urban agriculture projects popping up across Canada aim to cut the cost of fresh vegetables and fruit. In Toronto, The Stop's urban agriculture initiatives include an 8,000-square-foot garden at Earlscourt Park, a community garden at Hillcrest Park, a greenhouse, sheltered garden, and the Global Roots Garden at The Green Barn. These growing spaces yield over 4,000 lbs of fresh, organic produce annually. Community members working in them learn environmentally-friendly methods to grow fresh, local produce year-round.[239]

The City of Edmonton is also rethinking public spaces to make food more available to everyone. On July 19th, 2014, local volunteers joined the municipality[240] to plant more than 1,000 food-producing native trees and shrubs, including saskatoon bushes, high bush cranberries, currents, gooseberries, and pin cherries. Sustainable Food Edmonton,[241] a local charity, supports urban agriculture projects in the capital region and throughout the province of Alberta. Sustainable Food Edmonton projects outside the provincial capital include the Community Garden Project in Fort MacLeod, Kuusamo Girl Guides' Growing Green Neighbours Garden in Sylvan Lake, Community Food Connections Garden in Medicine Hat, as well as Rethink Red Deer's Spruce Edible Lane Forest Garden.

Community building and urban agriculture are good first steps to improving access to food for lower-income Canadians. But to eliminate the need for food banks in Canada, we must make a more fundamental change. We must change our attitude about food waste and the sustainability of our diets, as individuals, families, and businesses. While the poor go hungry, Canadians throw almost half their food in the garbage. We waste up to 40% of our food from field to the table, and most of that waste occurs in our kitchens. The loss amounts to $27 billion, or almost $800 for every Canadian.[242] That figure doesn't include fruit that goes wasted when homeowners and municipalities allow thousands of apples, pears, cherries, and grapes to rot on the ground because nobody bothers to harvest them, as happens year after year in southwestern Alberta.

Sadly, we've made food snobbery[243] a national pastime. For example, many food faddists throw out potatoes[244] as too calorie laden— in fact they are packed with nutrition with no more calories than an apple —and choose to eat expensive imported quinoa instead. That's a choice that causes hunger for people we don't see at the food banks, the rural population in countries like Bolivia.[245] It's an example of food snobbery at its worst. It is neither reasonable, sustainable or ethical.

Profiting from the Poor, a Growth Industry

It may satisfy our anxiety about being ripped off by the poor, but the way we provide the public with social, health and employment services in Canada wastes money, time, and human lives. Stressed and sick clients are assigned numbers. They wait for hours until that number is called so they can attend yet another pointless meeting. They pull their hair in frustration when yet another telephone call centre loop turns into a dead end. They give up getting help when bureaucrats ask them to complete forms complicated enough to confuse a lawyer. In short, the hoops and loops we create to weed out the undeserving poor do not manage human talent, do not raise the gross domestic product, and will not make Canada or its taxpayers richer. Perhaps the forest of bureaucracy is thickest in Alberta.

> For a year I have asked for help. I called the YWCA,[246] and couldn't get the outreach worker to understand me. When I went to Alberta Works, they insisted that I relive my trauma to a new stranger every time I walked through the door. No one seemed to comprehend the fact that I am a crime victim with a brain injury. Apparently, it happens all the time. *Notes, Spring 2014*

As I was picking apples off the ground, taking bottles back to the pop shop pay for dinner, and contemplating jumping off the bridge, the premier of Alberta, Alison Redford, was flying around the world on private jets and spending nearly $1 million on a private premier's penthouse palace[247] eleven floors above the provincial capital. Eventually, Alison's palace turned into a pile of rubble on top her political career, but the stinking system that makes it nearly impossible for people access government services stays in place.

This was the same provincial government that spent more than $21 million annually[248] on communications staff with an average of eleven communications staffers per ministry. This was the same government that expected welfare recipients to live on less than $600 per month. It was a government that felt entitled and destined to remain in power, even if everyday Albertans didn't agree.

On May 5, 2015, everyday Albertans finally told Alberta's Progressive Conservative government that they didn't agree. In a stunning turnabout, they threw out a Progressive Conservative party that no longer adhered to the progressive 'Red Tory' platform of Peter Lougheed, Alberta's first Progressive Conservative premier. They elected the social democratic New Democratic Party (NDP), led by Rachel Notley, to a majority government.

Many Albertans are hopeful their new government will completely rethink its participation in the poverty industry during its mandate. Cosmetic changes will not do. Still, in the summer of 2015 clients still waited for hours in queues to get questions answered when they could have been looking for a job or training for one. They still endured a triage system that made them wait for help until they had no food, medicine, or were about to be evicted from their homes on to the street. Sick people, trauma survivors, and crime victims still told their story over and over again to different workers every time they came in to a government office or called another part of the government's call centre octopus. Their only comfort? Knowing change might start by fall. Their biggest fear? That nothing would change.

It is clear from reading the Alberta Human Services[249] website that the department puts a lot of thought into its message. Positive language laces its purported mandate: "creating the conditions," "safe and supportive," "communities," and "opportunities to realize their full potential." Human Services views itself as a business that serves government, community partners, and stakeholders by delivering "citizen-centred programs and services that improve quality of life for Albertans." It's not clear exactly who all the stakeholders are, but it is clear that clients are not listed among the groups Alberta Human Services works with collaboratively. Civil servants appear to have forgotten that citizens of Alberta—including the people who walk into their offices asking questions or looking for help—are the people they should be serving.

Alberta Works[250] falls under the Ministry of Human Services.[251] It's the part of the ministry that provides money to people who have run out of EI, people struck by financial catastrophe like job loss, and the chronically poor. It keeps social exiles alive until they can be put to work, go back to school, or moved on to Alberta Income for the Severely Handicapped (AISH).

AISH recipients receive approximately triple the monthly benefit of Alberta Works recipients, but most of Alberta's sick, injured, and traumatized do not qualify for this program. Even those who do qualify find the process more complicated than applying to go to university. At best, applicants wait several months for acceptance. Often it takes several attempts over several years until an applicant is accepted as a client. In the meantime, the disabled person is expected to survive on social assistance, scrounge a living on part-time income, rely on family, or become homeless.

Front desks are still hard for me. I simply can't make the clerks understand. I am easily brushed off, or I walk out of the situation. It is hard to untangle a web in a single sentence, so hard. *Notes, June 2014*

I was in no shape to get help in the bureaucratic jungle. Getting help from Alberta Works requires a 'cool as a cucumber' attitude that keeps you from blowing your top when you're asked to tell your whole story over and over again to every worker you talk to in person or on the telephone. (What are they writing down in those computer files, anyway?) It requires the navigational skills of a jet pilot as you chart your way through the labyrinth of provincial call centres, answering machines, and voice messages. Unless you're bringing your own 'poverty industry worker' to advocate for you (or you've blown your top and threatened to write to the Minister), you'll need to wipe your schedule free as you wait in the waiting room of a Canada/Alberta Service Centre until your number comes up. When you're done, you'll probably need to book off still another day from your medical appointments, job-search, interviews, work (if you have a job), training, counselling, or family responsibilities. If you still have food in your fridge or a place to sleep, they'll probably put you back in the queue, and book you a follow-up appointment for a month from now. When you come back, you will be asked by a stranger to repeat everything that you told the first worker on your first visit. If you have great office administration skills, a personal assistant, and a fax machine you'll have a much easier time dealing with the bureaucrats. Sound ridiculous? It is. Am I exaggerating? Not if my experience is typical.

After spending a year navigating offices, waiting for appointments, dealing with telephone systems, and voice mail messages, I am convinced that Alberta Human Services is an octopus that strangles the dignity out of its clients, until they are limp enough settle for anything in order to escape the department's clutches. I am also convinced that old-style disdain for the poor dressed up as communicating and collaborating with stakeholder partners muddies what should be its true mission—serving citizens in their time of need.

Brain injured and traumatized, I spiralled down into suicidal ideation every time I dealt with Alberta Works.

> Today I got the supervisor's business card and a fax of my application to Alberta Adult Health Benefit. And I am to call if I need anything or if my income dips below $580.00 per month. But that took so much work. I almost died trying to get home.[252] *April 2014*

By February, I was back to skipping my thyroid medications for a few days until a column or demo job cheque came. I think it was the Head of Victim Services who told me that I should take the letter she wrote for me in to Alberta Works. So, I ventured into the bureaucratic forest one more time. This time I got past the reception area to meet with a young woman with dark brown hair, a perky attitude and a big smile. Since I was earning about $500-$700 per month from the demo job, she told me that I didn't qualify for help. She handed me a paper indicating benefits that I, as a victim of domestic violence, could qualify for. They included a bus pass, damage deposit and first month rent, full health and dental coverage including new eyeglasses (mine were being held together by tape). But since I was working part-time, I could not access these services. I learned later that they also would have paid for my transportation to see the neurologist in Calgary if I hadn't been working at all. But there is a bright spot. Eight months after my injury, and four trips into Alberta Works later, she tells me that I qualified for the Alberta Adult Health Benefit and should not be stretching my meds. Really? I have been doing it for years when money is tight. It's what poor people, especially the working poor, do in Canada.

Paying for prescriptions when you work part-time, on contract, or in a job without benefits, or for yourself can mean going without rent or dinner. It is one of the reasons the working poor[253] die sooner. A study funded by the Canadian Institute of Health Research found that one in three prescriptions go unfilled in Canada.[254] That means that instead of getting better or keeping chronic health conditions in check, millions of Canadians get sicker, miss work, and wind up disabled or dead, instead of contributing to the economy. According to the Centre for Policy Alternatives, a national pharmacare policy could not only improve lives of countless hard-working Canadians, it would save all of us taxpayers $107 billion a year.[255]

> Emailed AB Works last night, still no answer, still sick to my stomach and with the old wound on my head sizzling. I call Alberta Works about my prescriptions. I tell them my taxes are done, but I don't have my tax assessment yet. So, the Alberta Health Benefit cannot verify income. They told me to contact Alberta Works to have the emergency coverage extended. Later I get an email to call the Lethbridge office. A young man tells me my file is closed and gives me another number. I leave a message. No one is there. So, I call the line of the Alberta Health Benefit in Edmonton. The woman on the phone is nice, but she tells me that I need to call the emergency line. (That's a number I have already called.) She tells me no one will help me because I don't have young children. She tells me to wait until I have no food in my house and no medicine left. She tells me I probably don't qualify for help because I work. This is not what the website says I should do. It's not what I was told by AB Works at my appointment. By now, I am really sick. I am so tired of being told to be responsible. The suicidal thoughts—my plan to jump off the railway bridge—keep intruding. I can't make them stop. I will go to work tomorrow. It will be a relief from this. I am so sleepy now. I need to sleep. *Notes, April 2014*

So, why was I still waiting for my Alberta Adult Health Benefit card in April? It boils down to this. The province needed my Notice of Assessment from the Canada Revenue Agency (CRA) to determine my income in order to give me a permanent card. So, I called the CRA to help me sort out the family income mess I'd been left with when I was hurt. After several failed attempts to get somebody who understood what I was saying, I got a woman on the line professional enough to tell me exactly how to fill out the forms. After muddling through my books with a head injury, the CRA sorted out the rest. However, when I sent the Notice of Assessment to Edmonton, the province lost my application. And I lost it with Alberta Human Services.

It was the local supervisor who finally cleared up the mess. She gave me her business card, and said to call if I had any more trouble. The next time I called, she was out of the office.

About the same time I was sorting this mess, I got a bill from my doctor for a regular check-up. My husband had told Alberta Health Services (AHS) to cut me off provincial health insurance, apparently stating he didn't know where I was. Apparently, it is AHS policy to cut spouses off the family card at the request of their partners without attempting to notify the unsuspecting spouse that they no longer have coverage. As the woman on the phone explained it to me, it was clear that this policy made sense to bureaucrats even if it seemed ridiculous to people like me.

I spent another hour on the phone getting my health care card back. It got sorted, but my problem could have been worse if Alberta's PC government had followed the bidding of their base and re-instituted paid premiums in 2013.[256]

Back in the early 2000s, the Government of Alberta had a call centre filled with bill collectors who hassled the poor for hundreds of dollars a year in health care premiums. Families paid $1,056; singles $528. In 2008, the premiums as well as the call centre that hassled down-and-out Albertans for premiums they could not afford to pay were dumped as too regressive for Alberta Tories.[257]

If your boss paid your health care premiums for you, you probably didn't know you paid a provincial health care premium under the old system. But as soon as you fell into social exile, the government turned your already stressful life into a waking nightmare.

It's hard to say whether the Progressive Conservative rank and file, who voted to bring health care premiums back at their annual convention in November 2013,[258] understood what this regressive tax would do to real live Albertans. It's hard to believe party members cast their votes to bring it back knowing that collecting health care premiums from social exiles involved government minions phoning up newly unemployed, intermittently employed and self-employed people to threaten to cut them off provincial health care if they don't pay NOW.

I remember those calls well, back when I was living in a room above a bar in 2000, in poor health, trying to get back on my feet. It took months before one of the call centre minions turned away from the dark side long enough to tell me that I qualified for a premium exemption, and offered to send me an application form.

Even those exemption forms were a nightmare for many Albertans. Like the current Adult Heath Benefit Card, the premium exemption calculated family income based on the previous year's tax assessment. People facing an unexpected catastrophe—sudden unemployment, business failures, illness, family breakdown, emotional trauma, even injured crime victims—who were doing well financially when they filled out their tax return a year earlier were harangued until the bureaucrats could get their hands on a tax assessment that proved the person crying on the other end of the phone line had indeed had the bottom fall out of their life and was indeed having trouble surviving in the Promised Land.

Social Exile and the Law

Almost as soon as the stitches stopped the bleeding at the back of my scalp, people started telling me I needed to hire a lawyer 'right away' to protect my matrimonial rights. I had no food in my fridge and I could barely keep the lights on. I couldn't afford to pay a private lawyer to sort out my financial mess, let alone protect my rights. Even if I had qualified for Legal Aid, I was too sick to tell the story one more time. Chances are, they wouldn't have considered my case a priority anyway.

In June 2014, the *Edmonton Journal*[259] reported on a legal emergency. Suzanne Polkosnik, president and CEO of Legal Aid Alberta, told the *Edmonton Journal* that without an additional $12 million a year, the poorest Albertans could face "significant and potentially devastating" lack of access to legal help, The $12 million was needed to allow the society to raise Legal Aid income guidelines to allow the province's AISH recipients to qualify for Legal Aid, Polkosnik said. When it didn't come, Legal Aid closed six offices and laid off twelve staff.

Legal Aid funding from the provincial and federal governments had not grown in five years, and the system was $6.1 million shy of its 2015 obligations. The shortfall predicted to grow to $19.1 million in 2016. The result? Albertans were representing themselves in the courts, creating backlogs, or not defending their rights at all. During the height of the crisis, three low-income defendants walked free when a judge refused to prosecute defendants who did not have a lawyer.

Eventually, the flak from the province's lawyers and judges was too much for the province's Department of Justice. In July, after judges throughout the province ordered Legal Aid to represent eighteen AISH recipients in criminal matters, Alberta Justice came up with funding to cover the court orders, then promptly blamed the lack of funding for Legal Aid on Ottawa.[260] The additional funding was enough to keep the few AISH recipients judges had ordered Legal Aid to represent on the client list. But it wasn't enough to solve the bigger problem.

By October, the province had its fourth premier in three years.[261] Seeking to die down the controversy, Premier Jim Prentice[262] added $5.5 million to Legal Aid's annual budget. A crisis was averted in the criminal courts, but the additional funding did not give low income Albertans improved access to the civil courts. It remains to be seen if the current premier, Rachel Notley, will further expand Legal Aid coverage.

Across Canada, many law-abiding Canadians can't afford to access the courts. Defending your rights, from those included under the Charter of Rights and Freedoms to tenancy, from employment rights to family matters, has everything to do with your income bracket. In plain language, the poor cannot defend themselves against landlords, mortgage companies, medical malpractice, unjust dismissal or bill collectors.

Lack of legal power doesn't just make people poorer. Not being able to defend their financial and civil claims, the poor know that their so-called constitutional rights are just paper tigers. They embrace their identity as social exiles with no vested interest in the success of the community. To make matters worse, the apparent disdain of judges, bureaucrats, clerks, and bankers who 'assume' they know the story, along with smug self-satisfied attitudes of middle-class voters who assume there is a level playing field for all—including those who think we can recoup health care costs by hiring bill collectors to harass the poor for 'their fair share'—push social exiles toward cynicism. Who wants to contribute to a community that doesn't treat them fairly? Why vote, why work, why follow the law? No wonder crime and poverty are linked in the sociological data.

Murphy[263] declares that homelessness is explained by the 'lack of housing the poor can afford,' but it goes even deeper. Homelessness is rooted in lack of access to rights and services that are part and parcel with citizenship. Without the ability to defend civil rights, employment rights, property rights, matrimonial rights, custody rights, and landlord tenant rights, social exiles are left to drift to the bottom of the social heap. Social exile can even land you in jail.

There's a furor over whether convicted criminals should have to pay victim surcharges, to fund services to victims, but relatively little attention gets paid to the fact that in some jurisdictions the poor go to jail because they cannot pay fines for misdemeanours.

In the United States, prisoners often pay court costs, including the warrants used to arrest them. South of the border, members of America's underclass serve jail sentences because they cannot pay fines for minor infractions. One woman died in a cell because she couldn't pay fines imposed because she didn't send her children to school.[264] Another young man did time for catching a fish without a licence.[265]

In Canada, fewer citizens go to jail because they can't pay their fines, but law-abiding Canadians may find themselves under the thumb of Crown collection agencies. Among the most vulnerable are non-custodial parents without legal representation who can't meet their child support obligations, self-employed or intermittently employed citizens who can't pay regressive taxes, such as health care premiums, and citizens without funds to pay fines or civil judgements obtained against them by the Crown.

Government bill collectors may speed up the downward spiral of financially vulnerable citizens struggling, often without success, to meet financial obligations. For example the Government of Alberta confiscates refundable tax credits, including the Working Income Benefit (WITB) and WITB Disability Supplement, from low-income Albertans who owe money to the province, even if those taxpayers make regular monthly payments on their debt. These refundable credits are meant to help these low-income Canadians stay out of poverty.

The Poor Pay More

Nowhere does old-style blaming the poor for their predicament hold bigger sway than in the propaganda pushed at us by the financial services industry. The fear-and-greed based industry thrives on blaming the poor for being poor and scaring the middle class into buying its products. While saving for a rainy day is smart if you can swing it, financial planning cannot eliminate poverty. Many Canadians don't earn enough money to cover basic expenses, let alone buy what the planner is selling. Many more have too much debt for saving to make sense.

Three out of the top five reasons people fall into debt have nothing to with overspending. The top reason for debt is reduced income. Number two is divorce.[266] Poor money management comes in at number three. Underemployment is number four. Gambling is number five.

Those under financial pressure face expenses that their more financially secure neighbours do not. Surcharges and late fees on telephone and utility bills are justified as a way to make people responsible, but in reality they are just taxes on the poor. Poor customers often pay more to bank at a chartered bank. Most banks offer their wealthy clients accounts that waive service charges on high bank balances. They even waive overdraft charges for their better-heeled customers.

In most cases, the victims of banking policies that favour the rich suffer quietly, but in 2014, a medically discharged soldier got CBC's

Go Public to take Scotiabank to task after the financial giant charged him a $7,000 penalty fee when he was force to break his mortgage to return to his hometown.[267]

When they really get in a scrape, cash-strapped Canadians often head to quick-cash stores. These banking alternatives target low-income Canadians, but charge higher interest rates on loans than the chartered banks, as well as fees to cash paycheques, government cheques and gifts from family. In December 2014, Money Mart's short-lived campaign to turn gift cards into cash at a cost of 50 percent of their value sparked so much outrage across Ontario that it was cancelled.[268] Quick-cash stores' mercenary policies are prompting some municipalities to call for more provincial regulation to protect vulnerable Canadians.[269]

It's even hard for the poor to protect what they already have. Many of the poorest Canadians risk losing what they own in a flood or fire because they can't afford renter's insurance. And if that's not bad enough, middle-class Canadians may find themselves heading to the poorhouse (or its modern equivalent, the local homeless shelter) when insurers refuse to pay out after a flood or fire.[270] Insurance companies in Canada earned $4.4 billion in profits in 2012, a 24%[271] increase from 2011. It was surely enough to cushion them from their payouts for the Alberta Floods. They increased premiums anyway.

The cost of private car insurance causes even more stress for struggling Canadians. The Consumers Association of Canada (CAC) believes private auto insurance rips off Canadian consumers. They think that implementing a well-run public insurance system, modelled on Manitoba Public Insurance, in all Canadian provinces would provide Canadians with the best value on automobile insurance.[272]

An obvious solution to end the gravy train for insurance companies might include more affordable public transit, so people can to get to work without a private vehicle, as well as public car and home insurance plans throughout the county. Those initiatives might set the insurance industry and its political cronies howling, but they could help more of us find the Promised Land.

Social Exile and the Job Market

It is not only kids and part-time workers in economically depressed parts of the country that do not make a living wage. In southern Alberta, one quarter of workers make less than $15.00 hour. Province-wide, 21% of workers between the ages of 25–44 are low wage earners.[273] It's interesting to note that almost half of Canada's poor participate in the workforce.[274] Self-employed, part-time, intermittently unemployed, contract, seasonal, and low-wage workers line up at soup kitchens and food banks. Some even sleep on mats in homeless shelters. Why? They don't earn enough money to pay rent.[275]

Right across North America, employees work longer for lower wages, while Europeans work fewer hours and receive more social benefits. In March 2014, The British Broadcasting Corporation (BBC) interviewed Americans who resigned themselves to working as much as 60 hours a week with no overtime. One man quipped that this is the 'new America, more work for less pay.' Still, President Barack Obama faced stiff opposition from U.S. business leaders as he tried to use executive power to force companies to pay their employees for all the hours they worked.[276]

According to the Canadian Labour Congress, Canada has a record number of underemployed Canadians.

> Nearly five years after the end of the 2008–2009 recession, Canada's headline unemployment rate has remained fixed at 7.2% (December 2013), a level first reached mid-2011. But rather than a static group of individuals, large numbers of workers flow in and out of unemployment each month. Recessions affect these flows in various ways, for example fewer people quit their job or decide to enter the labour market when the job market looks dismal. Following a recession, there is usually an increase in the number of workers that are unemployed for extended periods of time… Since 2011 the number of underemployed workers has exceeded the number of unemployed workers—in 2013 there were 1.35 million unemployed workers and 1.43 million

additional underemployed workers. And that is before we even begin to take into account skills-related underemployment.[277] "Underemployment is Canada's Real Labour Market Challenge," Canadian Labour Congress, Thursday, 6 March 2014

In the 19th century, the working poor could always find a way to earn a few extra dollars. They could sell eggs, fruit, or garden vegetables in town, cut timber, help a neighbouring farmer, or get a job building the railway. Women could take in sewing, clean houses, or work as a hired girl.

Today, self-sufficiency and work ethic may not get you out of poverty. You'll need a business licence, health inspection, and zoning approval before you sell your home-grown produce or knock on the neighbour's door with your snow shovel, paint brush or ladder in hand. Even then, self-employment is no sure ticket out of poverty.

In the early 2000s, I did marketing work for small entrepreneurs, mostly in the food industry. Many of my customers earned less than they would have received on AISH or working at a minimum-wage job. They had no EI benefits to fall back on, no disability insurance, their pensions and retirement plans were in their businesses, and some had bill collectors hounding them.

Hugh, a rancher-turned-meat processor, always checked to see if I had enough of his beef in the fridge. And he never made me wait for payment, never quibbled about a bill.

I remember my last meeting with him. He was on to a new lead, getting good reviews from restaurant critics, selling into posh Calgary restaurants, on the brink, we hoped, of something big, maybe, finally. But I winced while he limped painfully across the parking lot to his truck. He often spent more than twelve hours on the road, getting in and out of that truck, puffing and wheezing, as he went looking for customers or investors.

He gasped for oxygen as he pulled himself behind the wheel. He coughed as he shut the door. I can't remember what I said, but I think it was something about him going home instead of to that next meeting. I do know he said something to the effect that he was just fine.

Lame, in his mid-fifties, overweight, with a heart condition, and out-of-control diabetes, he should have qualified for AISH, but he would never have applied. He was incapable of quitting. He was trying to save a lifetime of work, trying to build his pain into something to leave to his son, and losing.

Normally, I would hear from him almost every day. He always wanted updates on my work. But he didn't call the next day.

I phoned him when I was ready to have him review the promotional text I wrote after our meeting. No answer. I left a message, and another, and another. After a week of leaving messages, I called his twenty-something salesperson in Calgary.

"Oh, I am so glad you called," he said.

He paused, clearly scraping for the words. I grew anxious.

"I am very sorry." More silence. "I wanted to call you, but I didn't have your number, uhm..." He stumbled for the words, again. "Hugh died two days ago."

I don't remember the rest of the conversation.

Hugh's work ethic never gave out. His heart did.

CBC's *Exchange* natters on in the background. Amanda Lang is giving Canadians more guilt-inducing advice. I usually don't pay the show much attention. But then I catch the amply paid host saying that if you haven't saved enough for your retirement by the time you are in your mid-fifties, you'd better forego that round-the-world trip. I stop writing mid-sentence, grab the remote and switch the channel. Who is she kidding? If you are in your mid-fifties, and you haven't taken that trip, get on the road. Now! *Notes, Fall, 2014*

Working a Service Job

The quickest way to earn some cash is probably taking a gig in the service industry, but life as a customer service worker can border on the ridiculous. Have you ever arrived early at your local Walmart, to hear the sounds of cheering and chanting as soon as the automatic doors open? That is the staff finishing up their morning meeting, chanting like religious cult members.

The ride through the service world gets even crazier. Expect to find:
- Senior citizens, especially elderly women, among your co-workers. Most aren't working because they're bored; they're there because they can't buy groceries on their pensions.
- A series of gigs with part-time hours, little or no benefits, holidays or weekends off, or job security. Unless you get yourself into management pronto, you may need to work more than one job to pay your rent.
- Employees too frightened of winding up on the street to demand that their bosses adhere to labour law. "A Survey of Employment Standard Violations" completed by the Workers' Action Centre, in May 2011,[278] found that employees may be complicit in their own abuse out of fear. Others may exhibit Stockholm Syndrome-like behaviour, putting their bosses' best interests above their own.
- The upside, you will become an expert on human nature as you watch human beings, many in expensive looking outfits, who don't think anyone is watching, teach their carted children interesting behaviours like spitting and throwing garbage on the floor.

Unemployment remains at 7.0%,[279] but a significant number of Canadians are under-employed.

Canadians who want to improve their economic outlook by learning a skill face an uphill battle. Herb Emery, from the University of Calgary School of Public Policy and a fellow of the Fraser Institute found that Saskatchewan youth have a tough time getting apprenticeship training.[280] Excerpts from Emery's Saskatchewan-focused report indicate that apprentices are not sticking with their trade long enough to get their journeymen certificates, and that business and government need to invest in underemployed workers, especially young men. Emery points out that they are a group that is increasingly under-employed:

Saskatchewan has large numbers of residents who begin, but never complete apprenticeship training. The government has announced that it will fund additional apprenticeship training spaces in the post-secondary system, but what will it do to encourage higher rates of apprenticeship completion to increase the supply of qualified journeypersons? It may be that the government can do more for labour-market needs in the nearer term by considering policies like changing how technical apprenticeship training is delivered by post-secondary institutions; paying for full-time apprentice mentors; or paying apprentices during their technical training when they cannot work for pay.... Like most provinces in Canada, Saskatchewan has a large pool of underemployed males aged 15 to 24, many of whom have completed high school. In addition to recruiting labour from outside the province, more effort could be made to entice this particular underemployed group in Saskatchewan, particularly those beyond the ages reachable by guidance counsellors, into post-secondary trades training.[281]

Despite the fact that we are failing to train unemployed and under-employed Canadians for skilled work, some business owners insist they need temporary foreign workers because Canadians are too fussy to take jobs in their enterprises.

Some employers repeat the myth of a poor Canadian work ethic to justify their push to bring in temporary foreign workers. But look a little deeper. There is evidence that the push to bring in temporary workers is really about pushing wages and benefits down. A passive foreign workforce protects profits. Canadian workers who stand up for themselves cost more to employ.[282] Saskatchewan-based Houston Pizza even put their 'keep the workforce compliant' philosophy in a memo that warned temporary foreign workers against becoming 'Canadianized' and 'increasing their demands on employers.'[283]

Just as home children provided a steady supply of cheap vulnerable labour in the 19th and early 20th century, temporary foreign workers help employers maintain a submissive, desperate underclass of labour.

This underclass includes thousands of people born in Canada, who are too afraid to complain about low wages, unsafe working conditions, or workplace harassment. The threat of being replaced with a foreign worker keeps vulnerable Canadians in bondage, too.

According to Nesbitt Burns, the proportion of firms reporting a labour shortage is extremely low. "The skills mismatch in Canada has gained extraordinary prominence in recent weeks, with the Federal Budget highlighting the issue. Yet, the latest Bank of Canada Business Outlook Survey finds that only 25% of firms are reporting labour shortages—compared with a 15-year average of 35%. Even smoothing the latest two quarters (as in the chart) gives a below-average reading of 29% of firms."[284]

In March 2014, Canada's Parliamentary Budget Officer[285] agreed, "In an attempt to explain the continued weakness in the labour market, PBO examined indicators of labour shortages and skills mismatches but found little evidence in support of a national labour shortage or skills mismatch in Canada." The TD Bank concurred: "The notion of a severe labour market skills mismatch has topped the headlines. With data in hand, we debunk the notion that Canada is facing an imminent skills crisis."[286] So did the Alberta Federation of Labour.[287]

The conservative C.D. Howe Institute links the push for foreign workers with greater unemployment among Canadian workers:

> Canada eased the hiring conditions of TFWs several times, supposedly because of a reported labour shortage in some occupations, especially in western Canada. By 2012, the number of employed TFWs was 338,000, up from 101,000 in 2002, yet the unemployment rate remained the same at 7.2 percent. Furthermore, these policy changes occurred even though there was little empirical evidence of shortages in many occupations. When controlling for differences across provinces, I find that changes to the TFWP that eased hiring conditions accelerated the rise in unemployment rates in Alberta and British Columbia.
>
> The reversal of some of these changes in 2013 is welcome but probably not sufficient, largely because adequate information is still

lacking about the state of the labour market, and because the uniform application fee employers pay to hire TFWs does not adequately increase their incentive to search for domestic workers to fill job vacancies. *C.D. Howe Institute, Temporary Foreign Workers in Canada: Are they really filling labour shortages?*[288]

In August 2014, Alberta Federation of Labour President Gil McGowan wrote a letter to Alberta Human Services Minister Dave Hancock urging him to consider research by the Certified General Accountants of Canada, which demonstrated that skilled labour shortages in Canada are sporadic and mostly short-lived. His letter reads, in part:

Labour market projections are used to make important public policy decisions that have profound implications for working people and the economy. We cannot afford to get these calculations wrong because bad analysis leads to bad policy. And this isn't just a hypothetical problem. Inaccurate and misleading projections on labour shortages have already led to bad public policy such as the unjustified expansion of the Temporary Foreign Worker Program, the unnecessary changes that were made by the federal government to the age of eligibility for CPP and the punitive changes that were recently made to the EI system.[289]

According to Susan McDaniel, Canada Research Chair & Prentice Research Chair in Global Population and Economy, Prentice Institute, at the University of Lethbridge, Canada's so-called skills shortage is bogus.[290]

The Canadian Imperial Bank of Commerce (CIBC) also found that Canada has a large labour supply. While it agreed some skills shortages exist, the bank raised concerns that both skill shortages and labour shortages were misrepresented. It noted that industry-specific information was misinterpreted to make the case for a skill and labour shortage that could only be corrected with foreign labour.[291]

On June 20, 2014, Canadian workers who had been displaced by temporary foreign workers began telling the national press their stories.[292] Word also leaked out that government had found employers across the country breaking the rules.[293] With a few exceptions, Canadians across the political spectrum were outraged.

Minister of Labour Jason Kenney called a halt to the abuses. On June 20, 2014, Kenney cancelled the deluge of wage-lowering temporary workers, imposed limits on the number of workers allowed into the country, and upped the number of inspections at worksites.[294] He told employers to stop building their business models around a low-wage, complacent workforce of temporary foreign workers. "We will better prevent and detect abuse and penalize employers who abuse the program," Kenney said. "We will severely sanction those who break the rules. We'll better protect foreign workers and we'll also recognize that Canada benefits from international mobility."[295] He had a clear message to employers using the program to keep wages artificially low, particularly those in Alberta. He found their anti-labour stance incompatible with Conservative economic principles:

> So my message to them would be look, we're Conservatives. We believe in free markets. We don't believe governments should be distorting markets. And there should be a market response to the scarcity of a commodity like labour, and that market response, first and foremost, is higher wages. We don't see that in Alberta, the most extensive use of the program has been Alberta food services, 8 percent increase in median wages since 2006 versus 14 percent increase in CPI and 31 percent increase in overall provincial median wages. This is absolutely clear evidence that those heavy users of the program in that sector, in that province have, unintentionally, ended up distorting the labour market. We today are announcing no more distortions. *Jason Kenney, Canada's Minister of Labour, June 20, 2014*[296]

V
HACKING OUR WAY OUT OF THE WILDERNESS

When you are lost, you have to knock on a lot of doors to find anyone at home. *Notes, Spring 2014.*

Should auld acquaintance be forgot,
And never brought to mind?
Should auld acquaintance be forgot,
And auld lang syne!

(Chorus.) For auld lang syne, my dear,
For auld lang syne.
We'll tak a cup o' kindness yet,
For auld lang syne.

And surely ye'll be your pint stowp!
And surely I'll be mine!
And we'll tak a cup o'kindness yet,
For auld lang syne.
For auld, &c.

We twa hae run about the braes,
And pou'd the gowans fine;
But we've wander'd mony a weary fit,
Sin' auld lang syne.
For auld, &c.

We twa hae paidl'd in the burn,
Frae morning sun till dine;
But seas between us braid hae roar'd
Sin' auld lang syne.
For auld, &c.

And there's a hand, my trusty fere!
And gie's a hand o' thine!
And we'll tak a right gude-willie waught,
For auld lang syne.
For auld, &c.

Robert Burns, 1788.[297]

A LITTLE CUP OF KINDNESS (THE POLITICAL)

Will people really choose to be dependent if they have a choice? Will they stop creating when there is food in their bellies and no eviction notice on the door? Or is the creative impulse strong enough to keep them serving their communities, building families, constructing houses, making art, writing books and playing music, growing food, and inventing things, even when there is no threat of hunger? I am betting that it is. My experience tells me it is our negative attitudes that keep social exiles in poverty.

Our soup kitchens, shelters and handouts are no more a solution to poverty than putting crofters on ships or locking failed settlers in poorhouses were in the 19th century. Maybe it's time to offer our neighbours 'a cup of kindness.' Certainly the vulnerable could benefit from public servants who behaved like servants to the people—not their masters—who held themselves accountable not just to the politicians and deputy ministers, but to their clients, the people they should serve. Perhaps we could redirect public funding toward effective supports that do not traumatize social exiles, and do not take away their will to pull themselves up again the next time life knocks them down. Perhaps we should go further than that. Perhaps the kindest thing we could do is scrap the poverty industry and banish the bigotry, bureaucracy and judgment that hold it up.

In October 2014, York University and the Canadian Alliance to End Homelessness issued its *State of Homelessness in Canada* study.[298] Researchers concluded that an additional $46 per Canadian put toward affordable housing per year could drastically reduce homelessness.[299] They argued that increasing funding for affordable housing to $106 per Canadian would pay for construction of 8,800 new affordable housing units each year and finance a housing benefit for renters that would go directly to lower-income Canadians. The benefit would go out in installments throughout the year the way the Child Tax Credit does. Great idea, but let's not stop there.

A guaranteed annual income, also known as negative income tax, or guaranteed minimum income, would put even more money directly in the hands of low-income Canadians than social benefits do now, without forcing them to tell their stories to poverty-industry workers again and again, just to get a bag of groceries or keep the lights on. Every Canadian would have enough money to purchase their own food and accommodation, eliminating the need for food banks, homeless shelters, and all but emergency social service benefits.[300]

Wait a minute, say the critics. Won't paying people who don't work destroy the economy? Wouldn't giving people something for nothing feed entitlement culture? Wouldn't they just quit their jobs? Wouldn't society come to a standstill?

Well, that didn't happen in Dauphin, Manitoba, a Canadian community that became a laboratory for a guaranteed minimum income research experiment during the 1970s. Between 1974 and 1978, the federal government turned Dauphin into a four-year test site in which every family was guaranteed a minimum income through income tax redistribution. People did not quit working. They did not become addicts. They did not stop being responsible. Quite the opposite. Kids stayed in school longer, mental health improved, and fewer people wound up in the hospital.[301, 302]

There is a move to resurrect the campaign to give Canadians a guaranteed basic income. Basic Income Canada Network's BIG Push began in January 2014. Their March 2014 paper, *A Proposal for Reforming Social Security for Non-Elderly Adults in Canada*, outlines how the proposed program would work.

Basic Income Canada envisions an income-tested income transfer program that would be paid out through the income tax system. Citizens would receive cheques similar to a GST credit cheque. Under Basic Income Canada's proposal, minimum income guarantees could range upward from $11,258 to $43,030, depending on the program chosen. There would still be incentive to work, because a gradual clawback on earned income would be weighted to ensure all workers increased their income by working for wages in addition to collecting their guaranteed income. At the same time, workers on the edge of social exile would no longer be under the thumb of employers that exploited their vulnerability.

In his Fall 2014 Report,[303] the Auditor General of Canada, Michael Ferguson, urged politicians and civil servants to ensure their programs met the needs of citizens. Among his concerns were disabled veterans who have trouble cutting through bureaucratic red tape to access mental health therapy. He also pointed out evidence that northern Canadians may not be benefiting from federal subsidies intended to help northern retailers lower the cost of groceries. Ferguson wrote:

> One concern that I have in looking at these audits is that departments need to have a clearer understanding of whether the services they

are providing are truly meeting the needs of Canadians... The findings we have presented today, in particular in our audits of Veterans Affairs Canada, the Nutrition North Canada program and Library and Archives Canada, underscore the disconnect that happens when departments don't have a clear understanding of whether the services they are providing are meeting the needs of their clienteles. When departments do not fully consider the on-the-ground impact of their activities, they are missing opportunities to verify that they are hitting the mark for Canadians.[304]

The Auditor General's concern that programs aren't meeting citizens' needs might also be taken to heart by provincial and municipal governments, health care advocates, those who work with the unemployed, food banks, homeless shelters, and individual citizens.

We need to ask ourselves what we want our poverty industry to do. Do we want to shame the poor? Do we want a permanent class of social exiles? Do we want people on the low end of the economic spectrum to make choices about their lives?

Under a negative income tax system, individuals would have more money in their pocket. Canadians would not have to go begging for food or housing after personal catastrophes such as illness, injury, financial disaster, or trauma. They would be less likely to hide workplace violations and harassment in order to keep a paycheque. They would be in a better bargaining position to walk away from employers that used their fear of homelessness to exploit them. They would have at least some money to put toward getting trained for better-paying skilled careers. The shame-based poverty industry would be decimated, at long last.

A guaranteed annual income would help end social exile in Canada by giving the poor choices about how to spend their own money. Intrusive questioning that allows traumatized individuals to be re-victimized over and over again by the poverty industry would be eliminated. The biggest challenge to implementing such a massive change in income distribution lies not in the logistics of the plan, but in our attitudes about who the poor are and what our poverty industry is supposed to do. At the bottom of the decision is the question, "would we all be better off with a guaranteed annual income through the income tax system, than the myriad of inaccessible and complicated programs people have to squeeze themselves into now?"

Sure, it will cost money to end social exile, and Canadians are right to be concerned that another government initiative could prove expensive and wasteful. But we may wind up saving money by getting rid of the bureaucracy and waste in our current poverty industry. Consider this: poverty costs Canadians $72 to $84 billion every year as our hospitals overflow with social exiles experiencing physical disease, mental illness, and social isolation.[305]

If we decide scrapping our social services system is worth doing, we will also have to scrap our bigotry about people living in social exile. That won't come easily to many of us. But to completely reform the poverty industry, we'll need to get rid of our suspicions that the poor are taking advantage of us, and that tough love is the solution to trauma. We will need to make bureaucrats serve their clients, not powerful 'stakeholders' like business.

Maybe Canadians are not there yet. Maybe we are not ready to eliminate social exile because we still believe some people deserve their suffering. Maybe we do not want have to change our attitudes about who the poor are, or why they fall through cracks in our social safety net, and maybe we do not think it is worth trying to motivate the 'undeserving poor' into succeeding.

SCREAM LOUDER (THE PERSONAL)

> Boyle-in Guelph. On Saturday December 9, 1911, Barbara Gilchrist, Relict of the late William Boyle, aged 71 years, 6 months and 27 days…Simpson's Corners. Much sympathy to the Boyle family in the death of Mrs. Boyle at her daughter's home in Guelph last week, she being one of oldest residents of the community. *Fergus News-Record*, 14 December 1911, pp 4–5.

Barbara Gilchrist Smith Boyle died in the City of Guelph at her daughter Sophia Talbot's house. Sophia was the wife of Wilbert Talbot, nephew of Alberta Senator Peter Talbot. Wilbert's parents were long-time neighbours and old family friends.

Barbara did not choose her exile. She remained 'a native of Scotland' to her last day. But if Barbara did not make it home, she at least had good reason to think her children had reached the Promised Land. If we're not there yet, we owe it to her to keep trying.

Hardy Scots, like Barbara Gilchrist, were not diminished by their circumstances. They viewed them as temporary. Their vision for Canada, and for what they could accomplish as individuals, was not limited to the things that limit us: social science theories, political punditry and bureaucratic structures. The things that brought people out of the wilderness were the same things that keep people from being chewed up in the poverty machine today. They knew you had to take your place in the Promised Land, no one was going to give it to you.

Pre-Confederation colonists took possession of their Promised Land[306] by working non-stop sunrise to sunset. When my ancestors arrived in the Garafraxa district of Wellington county at the end of the 1840's, the Canada Company was no longer the only landowner selling cheap plots in the Huron Tract to British Subjects escaping potato crop failures, post-war recession, industrialization, and land clearances. There was a thriving real estate industry among people already settled in the province. Farms and bush plots were traded between farmers and absentee landlords, or sold to newcomers.

Not everyone rushing into the district got there on ships. Sons and daughters of soldiers who grew up on the Crown grants too small to support a second generation arrived ready to buy their own homesteads.[307] Americans not satisfied with opportunities in their young republic bought land, too. Small-time speculators, like the Gilchrists' neighbour Manasseh Leeson,[308] bought land from families moving out of the colony or who could not pay the mortgage.

No matter how difficult the journey, how desperate they were, how many times they had to start over, or how much money they hoped to make, colonists believed they could overcome obstacles in their way. They explored, homesteaded and thrived in business.[309] They bought land early and cheap, worked hard to turn bush into farmland, and had little patience with those who failed to establish themselves when the district was already settled.

Yet, they also knew how to help each other make it through another frozen winter. They knew there is no such thing as a self-made man. As Barbara Murphy writes in *On the Street: How We Created the Homeless*, "The real story is far less heroic. We make it with the help of our parents during our dependent childhood years, with the help of a teacher lifting us out of illiteracy and ignorance, with the help of the first employer who hired us when we had no work experience, and with some assistance from the hand of fate."[310]

Brené Brown writes in *The Gifts of Imperfection* that "one of the greatest barriers to connection is the cultural importance we place on 'going it alone.' Somehow, we've come to equate success with not needing anyone."[311]

On the other hand, it does matter what's inside of you—diminished expectations make us blind and unworthy to pursue opportunities, leading us to even more diminished lives. We are content to work harder for less.

The problem with the poverty industry is not that it encourages us to ask for help. The problem is that the poverty industry does not hear us when we call. And that it does not encourage us to get up again. Judgement about accepting help sickens the helper and the person who must accept inferior status to get help.

All the programs and policies that are supposed to help stop your fall through poverty to the streets exist on paper. But you can't reach behind the desk and catch the bureaucrat's attention for more than a minute or so. You have to screw up the hope from within you. You have to press on to get what you want. Even when you do not feel it, you have to press on, and on once more. That's hard to do when you are traumatized and living in social exile.

The reality I observed in my exile jarred me into realizing the dreadful incongruity between my experience and what I had been raised to believe. Canada is not the compassionate land of plenty I had been told it was. Hard work might not get you anything but broken dreams and a mat on the floor of a homeless shelter. On the other hand, pushing paper investments and foreclosing on mortgages of the unfortunate, or making windfalls in the real estate market can make you richer than Midas without any apparent downside, to yourself at least. I was jarred by the realization that no one was going to help me open the gate, that if I did not force that lock, that if I did not believe I was important enough to be helped, then the whole world would agree with me, and I would remain in exile. I had to force the lock out of my isolation, even though I did not feel like it. But an ancient toughness lives in me. Dour determination, stiff upper lips, and a wandering spirit sail together on the current of my veins.

The poverty industry (aka the welfare culture) pulls you down and away from who you are and your belief that you can accomplish anything significant. Once you let them take you in hand, if you have ever had ambition or a dream, you lose it. Instead, you morph from a competent person with a vision for your life to a hopeless bowl of jelly juggling in lumps this way or that, according to the whims of visionless bureaucrats and helpers who myopically gaze at their rule books, barely making out the shape of the bedraggled person in front of them, let alone apprehending the gift or mission that is central to that person's humanity. You are as indentured as the crofter was before he left the estate and as oppressed as the textile worker before he escaped the mill.

Even as I floundered, with a brain that wouldn't work and the financial mess my husband left me to unravel, even as I contemplated putting on my coat and walking toward the railway bridge that carried me to this city in my teenage mother's belly—she screaming all the way at how high it was—the stubborn wilderness walker in me insisted on chopping yet another log for the fire, writing one more sentence, holding one more garage sale, going out one more time to collect bottles and gathering fruit that my prosperous neighbours let rot on the ground.

I learned that it was not 'all my fault,' but that I could not count on our messed-up 'poverty industry' to keep me off the street, let alone get me to the Promised Land. I learned that, sometimes, you just have to set out to sea, and try your luck in a new frontier. Follow sheer gut instinct. Move toward something. Take a risk, rather than standing there freezing and starving. Do something, even if that something is only asking for help. Keep ploughing your way free until those snowdrifts are behind you. Don't let them convince you that it's you, not the system, that's the problem. Ask for what you're entitled to. It is your birthright. But don't depend on them giving it to you.

I learned this too. Entitlement is not all bad, and there are rights of citizenship. The people paid to help you are supposed to give you what you are entitled to, and don't let them tell you any different. Even social exiles are entitled to dignity, food, shelter, health care, and respect. 'Do Gooders' who tell you not to be angry, to move on when you are still bleeding, that your cuts and your hunger are no big deal, the ones who walk past you in their leather boots while you stand shoeless in the snow, are not good at all.

In the midst of my pain, I scribbled this on a piece of paper: "One day you will be ready. You will take your catastrophes out to look at them again and feel no pain; your trauma, disappointments and sheer bad luck will lose their power, and the pain will vanish. You will see all that your exile has taught you. It is only then that you can forgive. To do it any earlier is just to bury pain and resentment and lie to yourself." I added this after I moved into my apartment: "Now it's time for you to embrace everything you learned in your exile and try to change the world, a little at least. It is all an assignment."

Above all, I learned that I had to take the Promised Land. No one, not even the people paid to help me would hear me unless I screamed louder.

WHEN WHAT YOU WISH ISN'T WHAT THEY WANT

When I was 21, I followed my first husband to British Columbia. Before our eldest son was born, I walked pregnant along the beach beside Okanagan Lake every afternoon, until I found my bench facing the wind and water. There I sat filling up empty journals with my stories and post-teenage angst. One day, two young men in Bermuda shorts and striped T-shirts walked by and asked if I was writing a book. I was embarrassed by their question. Who was I to write a book, even if it was my secret dream? *Notes, Spring 2014*

In April 2014, I went to Calgary for psycho-neurological testing at the Foothills Hospital. It was mid-June by the time the psycho-neurologist called me with her assessment, and I hoped for answers. Why was I still leaving water running in the sink; still panicking when the phone rang; still able to work only a few hours a day; still exhausted? Why did my head feel like my skull was cracking open when I worked too long? Why did pain shoot from my spine into my skull? How was I to bridge the summer gap between my empty bank account, and the money I had coming in September?

The test results pinpointed some problems. The psycho-neurologist referred me to a brain injury support agency in Lethbridge. They sent a letter to my doctor, saying rehabilitation might help. Could this be the rope that pulled me to shore? I hoped so.

> Are we finally getting somewhere? One of the neurologists called yesterday with the results from my testing. Today, the social worker from the Foothills followed up with a referral in Lethbridge. At last help. *Notes, June 18, 2014*

It was another week before I heard from the rehabilitation worker. A few days later, she came to my house, saw the state I was in, and decided rehabilitation could wait. I needed food in my fridge, I needed money in the bank, and I needed a place to live when the house sold. She moved quickly. In no time, I had an appointment with an employment agency for people 'with barriers to employment,' a written note from my doctor, and a card from the food bank. But there were hints that I would have to chuck my writing, give up my dog and live in a room somewhere. The relearning strategies the psycho-neurologist recommended did not materialize.

This didn't feel right. For a year, I'd hoped for help from the province. Now I had it, and it terrified me. I felt myself falling down under the weight of labels—being sucked into the poverty industry. I did not like this feeling, but I was grateful for the food.

> There's food in my pantry, but I am trapped. I find myself spiralling down, into something worse than poverty, giving up my independence; that I must accept less because I am broken. *Notes, July 19, 2014*

The rehabilitation worker and I went to Alberta Works again. She wanted to sign me up for income support. I didn't want to be there. I told my worker that I would rather sell the furniture than go back to that building. She told me I shouldn't have to do that. Even as we sat there, I thought about leaving before my name was called, but I chatted with the worker instead. She said it would be fine.

> We go behind the grey partition into a row of cubicles. A bureaucrat I have never seen before tells me to sit in the chair in front of her grey cage. She starts asking questions I have answered a dozen times

before. She wants me to retell every difficult detail of this whole horrible year one more time, justify why I am sitting there in front of her.

My throat stops. My mind goes blank. I can't get the words out. I want to go home. I would rather sell the furniture and eat dandelions than tell this story one more time to bureaucrats who haven't earned the right to see my pain.

The searing pain shoots up my neck and cuts off my brain again. The back of my head feels like the bolas is splitting it open again. By now my words are slurring and I feel an electric current running though my head. Shaking, I shout, "I am not telling you people this again. It's all in your computer."

The worker sputters, "I have to ask."

"No, you don't. Get me a supervisor, or I will be at Weadick's[312] office in five minutes." I push my papers back inside my bag. I start to leave. For the first time in months, I am a chooser, not a beggar. The wide-mouthed rehabilitation worker looks horrified at the thought of me trotting over to tell Greg Weadick, then Alberta's Minister of Advanced Education and Technology, why Alberta Works wasn't working for people like me.

"OK, I'll get you a supervisor. Five minutes," says the stunned bureaucrat.

> The brain injury worker takes me outside until I stop shaking. When we get back in, the supervisor is there. She digs up my file. She takes the note from my doctor that says I have injuries and can only work part-time. She tells me where I can get my hearing checked. She says to replace the eyeglasses that hang together with tape. I have money by Friday. *Notes, August 20, 2014*

It's not the first time I have panicked in a poverty-industry office. I have felt pressured to give up my teaching and writing, and to take a minimum-wage job for weeks now. A few weeks earlier I was pushed into registering at a job placement agency for disabled people. At intake, they wanted my history. I had to tell about the beating again.

Once more I descended into dizziness and panic, unable to remember what to say next, stumbling over my tongue, unable to answer the worker's questions.

I am awaking in fear again. Thinking someone may be in the room. Ghosts—this house is empty with ghosts—broken dreams reminding me how much we loved this place—gone with the one I hoped to share them with. The poverty industry has finally encapsulated me. I am losing my dignity. I am spiralling down, tumbling through the social safety net into the water below. I must pull myself to shore.

Realistic hope, what is that? I sit in the wingback chair, silent, sinking to the depths of my brain. Some would call it meditating; others praying. I have money in my wallet from a garage sale. I can pay a bill or two, buy dog food, take the bus, and eat meat myself this week. I can have milk on my oatmeal, and coffee with sugar in the morning. I have a box full of teabags. I am more grateful than the situation calls for. I see the end of this long summer of misery, realizing I have just a couple months more until I navigate myself out of this place of haplessness, before last year's flood is over for me. Fall will bring the cool breeze of choice.

My perspective turns on its head.

I'm holding a copy of Malcolm Gladwell's *David and Goliath, Underdogs, Misfits, and the Art of Battling Giants* in my hands. I've borrowed it from the library. I open it. The first page confirms what has been brewing in my brain for the last week.

I don't know how, but I have accessed a powerful, unbroken room inside my head. In a split second, I don't care what 'they' think anymore. I stop seeing my spiral of struggle as pure disaster. I perceive it as another assignment. It is the beginning of my understanding that I am injured, not weak. There will be a way to get where I need to go, and that I won't be one of the 'undeserving poor' if I say 'no' to other people's plans for me. I practice saying no to well-meaning people who have plans for me, who think they know what I should do, and where I should go.

Labels are not a roadmap. I have stories to tell.

When I get to church, I listen to the story of the loaves and fishes again. The woman across the aisle is crying. Her son has died. Another young man weeps near the altar. I have not noticed others for a long time.

I have been too tired too move. Until now. I would rather sleep in the bed I was choked on; beside the wall my open scalp smeared red, in front of the closet my crimson river ran down, toward the bloody handprint on the carpet I made grasping at the floorboards, than sell the bed and pack my drawers. I have been here for more than a year, stuck in the past without any promise of a future. So long that I've almost fooled myself into thinking of this mausoleum of despair as home.

Now, it is time to move, but where do I begin? How did we accumulate so much stuff in our disaster-upon-disaster-ducking marriage? I clean it up alone. I begin packing for the move before the house is sold, unsure where I am going, but knowing that I must go.

> I am at Safeway. The executive director of a non-profit I used be a board member of is shopping, too. Across from the yogurt and cheese, she says she is glad I did not jump off that bridge last winter. I tell her I am glad, too. *Notes, Late August 2014*

In late September, my mother comes to visit me. She and I sit on the couch and watch movies. For the first time since I was about seven I spend time alone with her. Just as we did when I was six, and she pulled me out of bed late at night to keep her company, watching her sew my school clothes for grade one. She used to take me to prayer meeting with her on Wednesday nights when the others were too little, until we both realized she didn't like who I was and what she thought I kept her from. I've always felt guilty about what my birth meant to her, deferred dreams of university and career, and a life she never seemed to want. Eventually, she salvaged her dreams, and perhaps her mother's, too. Grandma beamed when she talked about how my mother went to university at fifty, won scholarships, and then got a government job. But I never got over feeling guilty for being; driven to excel not for myself, but to make my presence on earth worth the trouble I caused.

I am not free yet. I am afraid that if my injury payment does not come before I leave the house, the poverty industry will force me to give away my dog, break my writing contract and quit teaching my fall workshops. All night, I reel at the thought of being subsumed into the poverty industry. But I wake up knowing what to do. I type 'financial help for writers in Canada' into the search engine on my dying netbook. Writers' Trust of Canada appears on the screen, and though cold fear stabs my heart I print out the application form. My heart still pounding with dread of hearing another 'no,' I ask my colleagues in Ontario and Alberta for references. Within hours, I have three 'yeses.' The Writers' Trust sends me a cheque quicker than I can work myself into an anxious fret.

I do the thing I really want to do.

I call Alberta Works and tell them I don't need them anymore. They are ecstatic. Most people don't call back in three weeks to say they don't need them anymore.

I finish my book one small section at a time. Sometimes, I bring my laptop to dinner at a McDonalds for the free coffee refills, Wi-Fi, and cheaper-than-I can-make-at-home bacon burgers. Sure, there are screaming children and parents threatening to stick their fingers in their kid's yogurt and eat their fries. But I am happy. I am alive. I am working. Who could afford to write a whole manuscript at Starbucks, anyway?

Since no one will do it for me, I create my own workplace accommodation so I can teach again—printing notes with heading-size type for my fall writing workshops, shortening my lectures, tripling the number of exercises. The students don't know why I've changed my style, but they tell me they like the format. I am still not all better, but I know I don't need to settle for work the poverty industry slots me in.

I think maybe I can do this. Maybe there will be a next book, a next article, a next workshop. I drink green tea, fix a salad, walk my dog and grab all the beauty I can to fix my soul. I press my doctor for answers. He books an MRI and tries to find me another specialist. When that falls flat, I find another doctor. We begin again.

I find the note I scribbled in September, when I harvested the tomatoes on the deck.

> The tomatoes are nearly finished, and I wish I had planted potatoes. I should have planted potatoes. *Notes, September 2014*

I wish I had not let fear make my garden too small. By Hallowe'en I am gone.

VI
FINDING HOME

The train has not stopped by, but I can see the station in the distance. I need to take a train ride. Notes, March 2014.

Exile changes you. It's not where you go in the wilderness, but that you do go. You realize that all the stuff and status you thought you needed really never counted for much in the long run. Home is no longer the place you settle in, but the journey you take to get there.

Finding home is insisting on your right to decide, and not allowing yourself to be diminished by opinions, restrictions, labels or incompetence, yours or other people's. That does not mean that you can ignore the work of changing the world or that those time-wasting bureaucrats should not be held accountable for making your journey harder. It means that they cannot stop you on your journey. It makes your winters in the wilderness worthwhile.

> Uncertainty is OK. We have little else to choose from. *Notes, June 22, 2014*

Barbara looks back at me from the photo that sits on the mantle in my new apartment, reminding me that I am not the first woman to wind up in a wilderness she never hoped to be in, and that ours is not the first generation to walk past the poorhouse. Maybe genes, history, and the circumstances of my birth made me more vulnerable to falling through the social safety net. Maybe I was born an outsider. No doubt trauma runs in my blood. Even if all that's true, I was born strong enough to overcome the wilderness. Dreams, creativity, and success run stronger than failure in my inheritance.

I learned how to draw water from a well before I learned to write my name. As the blazing summer sun stung our eyes, Grandma[313] taught me to prime the pump with the last water from the pail, then to place the empty pail below the spout to draw a drink from the icy stream hidden below us.

Wells are fine when there is no open water. But I like to see water flow, as long as it is small water trickling over the stones in a brook or a city fountain, containable water; not the rushing, drowning flood that wipes us away like the gophers in the sludge. I love to gather shells along the shore or take the ferry to Victoria, but I am afraid to swim in the ocean.

I pick up the notes I scribbled on the anniversary of my injury.

> Exactly one year ago today, we filled water bottles in anticipation of the flood. This morning I emptied them on the lawn and houseplants, so that I can return them for the $40 deposit. Tipping over the patio onto the lawn, they trickled and spiralled like garden fountains, gurgling like artificial brooks, sparkling in the sunshine. The river is high again tonight, like it was last year, fascinating and frightening, harmless looking and silently rising to the top of the bridge. And my anxiety is rising with it. I am afraid of drowning in helplessness.
>
> We need to live by the water, we humans. But I am a prairie girl; I grew up knowing how to suck a living out of the miserly earth; and I have spent my life walking on cracks the water left in the parched black clay. *Notes, June 21, 2013*[314]

I am tired of thirst, stale water, and false promises. I have little patience for what are often called first-world problems, and well-fed spoilt brats who chatter loudly over their cappuccino steam about what they know the poor should do to improve their lives, "It's THEIR thinking that's messed up, you know." The pompous do-gooders of the left and the sanctimonious tough lovers on the right are equally out of answers. Most of their programs are simply ways to assuage the consciences of middle-class folks who wouldn't dream of implementing solutions, like a guaranteed annual income or teaching people to grow their own food, or eliminating bureaucratic traps and income hurdles that destroy human souls. No matter what they say, they still believe that the poor are mostly undeserving of help.

If I lose the place where I lay my head or never again know the warmth of a full bank account, it will not be for want of trying to take care of myself. Still, I cannot accept the narrow vision of the bureaucrats anymore than my ancestors accepted the narrow vision of estate managers or Presbyterian pastors who wanted them to be content with their lot and conform to roles and diminished expectations. Too many have ploughed their way out of the wilderness on my behalf for me to ever accept that.

I craved certainty, but I learned that certainty is slavery to the little story, the perpetual poverty of a diminished vision, just getting by. Had I given in to what was expected, I would have a little room, wearing labels instead of dreams, without my dog, doing a suitable job for a brain-injured victim of domestic violence, or worse yet, living on handouts while workers told me what I could not do anymore.

I don't know why we so easily cast dreams into the fire and repeat the failures of those who went before us. Sometimes, I still shout 'why' to the silence when I am alone. I may never stop demanding the universe change its order to accommodate me.

I tell the do-gooders and the tough-lovers alike: "You want me to tell a story that is not my own—fit into what you think I am supposed to be. But I am full of lilacs and wildflowers, and I will tread upon the earthy stones and waterfalls, not pavement and tiles. I cannot be what I am supposed to be, what you want me to be. I cannot twist and squeeze myself into a shape to fit this drone-a-day, workaday world. I cannot make myself little enough for you."

I dance barefoot along the shore, get my feet wet skipping between stones in the ice cold river, though broken bottle glass cuts my heel. I feast upon berries, though mosquitoes sting. I pick wild Alberta roses, though thorns prick blood from my grasping fingers. And I let the wind and rain and hail pelt my skin and hair as I run for shelter, never wishing I had stayed inside. This is home.

BIBLIOGRAPHY

Books and Articles

Aberdeen Digital Living. *Along the Garafraxa Trail* (History DVD Ebook), Part 4), Aberdeen Digital Living.com Garafraxa Trail, http://www.aberdeendigitalarchiving.com/garafraxatrail.htm

The Aboriginal Justice Implementation Commission, The Justice System and Aboriginal People, Accessed: http://www.ajic.mb.ca/volumel/chapter4.html

ACE Study. "The Adverse Childhood Experiences Study," ACE Study.org http://www.acestudy.org.

Alberta Civil Liberties Research Centre. "What is Access to Justice, Five Different Views?" Accessed at http://www.aclrc.com/what-is-access-to-justice/ 20 December 2014.

Alberta Communication Staff Cost of $23 Million. *The Huffington Post Alberta*, 04 April 2014. Accessed: http://www.huffingtonpost.ca/2014/04/04/alberta-communications-staff_n_5091565.html

Alberta Federation of Labour. "Alberta relying on bogus labour-shortage figures (analysis of the government's methods)," News Release, Accessed: http://www.afl.org/index.php/Press-Release/alberta-relying-on-bogus-labour-shortage-figures.html

Alberta Federation of Labour. "New study on labour market shows that there is no widespread labour shortage," News Release, Accessed: http://www.afl.org/index.php/Press-Release/low-wage-employers-in-alberta-are-blowing-smoke-when-they-whine-about-labour-shortages.html

Anderssen, Erin. "What is the best city to live in if you are a woman," *The Globe and Mail*, 22 April 2014 Accessed: http://www.theglobeandmail.com/life/relationships/what-is-the-best-canadian-city-to-live-in-if-youre-a-woman/article18110103/#dashboard/follows/

Archives Society of Alberta."Lethbridge Nursing Mission," *Alberta On Record.* http://www.albertaonrecord.ca/lethbridge-nursing-mission.

Azvolinsky, Anna. "Pregnancy Stress Spans Generations," *The Scientist,* August 7, 2014. http://www.the-scientist.com/?articles.view/articleNo/40716/title/Pregnancy-Stress-Spans-Generations/

Babad, Michael. "How speculators fed u.s. housing bubble, fuelled bust," *The Globe and Mail,* Friday, Dec. 16 2011. Link: http://www.theglobeandmail.com/report-on-business/top-business-stories/how-speculators-fed-us-housing-bubble-fuelled-bust/article4197115/.

Bailyn, Bernard. Voyagers to the West, A Passage of in the Peopling of America on the Eve of the Revolution. Knopf Doubleday, 1986, p. 61.

Bartlett, Randall and Helen Lao. Labour Market Assessment 2014, Office of the Parliamentary Budget Officer, 25 March 2014 http://www.pbo-dpb.gc.ca/files/files/Labour_Note_EN.pdf

The Big Push. "The Big Push of Basic Income Canada," The Big Push.net Accessed at http://www.thebigpush.net, December 2014.

BMO Chief Economist, BMO Capital Markets. "Skills Shortages? We've Seen Worse...Much Worse," BMO Nesbitt Burns, April 2, 2013. Accessed at http://www.bmonesbittburns.com/economics/amcharts/apro213.pdf

Broughton, J.W.D. *They Desired a Better Country.* Brighton, Ontario: J. Broughton, 1981.

Brouwer, Ruth Compton. *New Women for God: Canadian Presbyterian Women and India Missions, 1876–1914.* Toronto: University of Toronto Press, 1990.

Brown, Brené, Ph.D. LMSW, *Daring Greatly, How the Courage to be Vulnerable Transforms the Way We Live, Love, Parent, and Lead.* Gotham Books, 2012.

Brown, Brené, Ph.D. LMSW, *The Gifts of Imperfection, Let Go of Who You Think You're Supposed to Be and Embrace Who You Are.* Hazelden, New York, 2010.

Brown, Jennifer. *Canadian Lawyer Magazine,* Legal Feeds, Legal Aid Alberta gets more money but challenges remain: chairman 11 August 2014 http://www.canadianlawyermag.com/legalfeeds/tag/legal-aid.html

Brown, Right Reverend Dr. Terry, Bishop of Malaita, Church of Melanesia, Transcriber. "2007 Project Canterbury, Mission to Rupert's Land," *From the Colonial Church Chronicle and Missionary Journal, Vol. IV* (January, 1851) pp. 247–252. Accessed at http://www.anglicanhistory.org/indigenous/budd/mission1851.html

Brown, Steven J. and Krista A. "Reading," *East Garafraxa, A History, The Corporation of the Township of East Garafraxa,* 2006.

Burleton, Derek,Vice President and Deputy Chief Economist; Sonya Gulati, Senior Economist; Connor McDonald, Economist; Sonny Scarfone, Research Associate. "Jobs in Canada, Where, What and For Whom," TD Bank, October 22, 2013. http://www.td.com/document/PDF/economics/special/JobsInCanada.pdf

Burns, Robert. "For Auld Lang Syne," 1788, Accessed at Robertburns.org http://www.robertburns.org/works/236.shtml

Burrows, Auger, Roy, and Alix. "Socio-economic inequalities in suicide attempts and suicide mortality in Québec, Canada, 1990–2005," Public Health 124, Feb 2010, Public Health 124, pp. 78–85.

Cambridge Advanced Learners Dictionary & Thesaurus © Cambridge University Press http://dictionary.cambridge.org/dictionary/british/talk-through-your-hat.

Campey, Lucille H. *An Unstoppable Force, the Scottish Exodus to Canada.* Natural Heritage Books, 2008.
Pp. 168–169.

_____. *The Scottish Pioneers of Upper Canada, 1784–1855: Glengarry and Beyond*, Natural Heritage Books. May 16 2005

_____. *After the Hector, The Scottish Pioneers of Nova Scotia and Cape Breton, 1773–1852*, Second Edition. Natural Heritage Books. 2007.

Canadian Centre for Policy Alternatives. "National pharmacare plan could save up to $10.7 billion a year: study," News Release,13 September 2010, Accessed at http://www.policyalternatives.ca/newsroom/news-releases/national-pharmacare-plan-could-save-107-billion-year-study.

Canadian job market increasingly a tale of have and have not occupations: CIBC, CNW, Toronto, December 3, 2012. http://www.newswire.ca/en/story/1082363/canadian-job-market-increasingly-a-tale-of-have-and-have-not-occupations-cibc

Canadian Labour Congress, "Underemployment is Canada's Real Labour Market Challenge," 6 March 2014. http://www.canadianlabour.ca/news-room/publications/underemployment-canadas-real-labour-market-challenge

Canadian Nurses Association. Contribution to Reducing Poverty in Canada Brief to the House of Commons Standing Committee on Human Resources, Skills and Social Development and the Status of Persons with Disabilities (HUMA) Ottawa, Ontario June 10, 2009,Canadian Nurses Association Accessed at http://cna-aiic.ca/~/media/cna/page-content/pdf-fr/reducing_poverty_e.pdf Federal

Canadian Oxford Dictionary, editor Alex Bisset, Oxford University Press, Don Mills, Ontario, 2000.

Cash, Rick, Murat Yukselir, and Jerry Johnson. "Time Machine, What life was like in Canada before the First World War." *The Globe and Mail*, 26 June 2014, 2:03 PM EDT, Updated 11 November 2014, 2:48 PM EST.

"Castle gives up swastika secret," *The Scotsman*, 9 August 2008.

CBC News. "Legal Aid Funding to Increase in Alberta. Province Commits More Money and will increase upper limit for eligibility," 30 October 2014. http://www.cbc.ca/news/canada/calgary/legal-aid-funding-to-increase-in-alberta-1.2818806

Centre for Non-violence and Social Justice, "What is Trauma?" Nonviolenceandsocialjustice.org, Accessed at http://www.nonviolenceandsocialjustice.org/FAQs/What-is-Trauma/41

Cheney, Peter. "Why Ontario Drivers Pay the Highest Car Insurance Rates in the Country," *The Globe and Mail*.Wednesday, July 09 2014. http://www.theglobeandmail.com/globe-drive/adventure/trends/why-ontario-drivers-pay-the-highest-car-insurance-rates-in-the-country/article19522860/?click=sf_globefb#dashboard/follows/?click=drive

Cheshire, Tom. *The Explorer Gene: How Three Generations of One Family Went Higher, Deeper and Further Than Any Before,* Marble Arch Number, cited in *National Geographic*, article by David Dobbs, Restless Genes." January 2013 http://ngm.nationalgeographic.com/2013/01/125-restless-genes/dobbs-text

Citizenship and Immigration Canada. "Subject/Sujet: Minister for Employment and Social Development Jason Kenney and Minister of Citizenship and Immigration Chris Alexander Hold a News Conference to Make an Announcement on Reforms to the Temporary Foreign Worker Program." Transcription/Transcription News Conference/ News Conference/Conférence De Pressed; Date/Date: June 20, 2014, 1:30 p.m. Location/Endroit: National Press Theatre, Ottawa, Principal(s)/Principaux: The Honourable Jason Kenney, Minister of Employment and Social Development and Minister for Multiculturalism; The Honourable Chris Alexander, Minister of Citizenship and Immigration.

CKOM. "Family identifies remains found in burned car in Prince Albert," NewsTalk, CKOM.com Accessed at http://ckom.com/category/region/prince-albert

Cohen, Mary Griffin. "Decline of Women in Dairying," *Histoire Sociale/Social History*.

Collin, Chantel, Political and Social Affairs Division, Parliament of Canada. "PRB 07-22E Poverty Reduction in Canada—The Federal Role," Parliament of Canada, 23 October 2007 Accessed at http://www.parl.gc.ca/Content/LOP/researchpublications/prb0722-e.htm 5:02:19/03/2014

Community Food Centres Canada. "Mapping the Possibilities of Food, "Community Food Centres Canada, 2013–14 Progress Report," December 2014, Accessed at http://cfccanada.ca/sites/default/files/documents/CFCC_2013-14ProgressReport_FINAL_web.pdf

Conway, Rebecca and Shah Imtiaz. "For Some in Pakistan Suicide the only way to escape poverty," *National Post*, 14 Feb 2012, http://news.nationalpost.com/2012/02/15/for-some-in-pakistan-suicide-the-only-way-to-escape-poverty/

Crawford, Cameron. "Disabling Poverty and Enabling Citizenship: Understanding the Poverty and Exclusion of Canadians with Disabilities," Community–University Research Alliance between the Council of Canadians with Disabilities and University of Victoria for the Community–University Research Alliance between the Council of Canadians with Disabilities and University of Victoria, http://www.ccdonline.ca/en/socialpolicy/poverty-citizenship/demographic-profile/understanding-poverty-exclusion.

Cryderman, Kelly. "Almost a year after the Alberta flood, housing market yet to recover," *The Globe and Mail*, April 27 2014.

CTVNews.ca Staff. "Outrage after Montreal store lays out spikes to deter homeless," 10 June 10, 7:55PM EDT http://www.ctvnews.ca/canada/outrage-after-montreal-store-lays-out-spikes-to-deter-homeless-1.1862513

Dryden, Ken. Special to the *Star*, "Edited interview with Nick Saul, president of Community Food Centres Canada, former head of The Stop," *Toronto Star*. Mon Jun 30 2014/ http://www.thestar.com/news/gta/2012/05/12/rethinking_the_food_bank_its_no_longer_just_about_handing_out_food_to_the_hungry.html

Dupere V, T Leventhal, and E Lacourse. "Neighborhood poverty and suicidal thoughts and attempts in late adolescence," Dupere V, Leventhal T, Lacourse E. Psychol Med. 2009, http://www.ncbi.nlm.nih.gov/pubmed/18845013

Emery, J. C. Herbert, Department of Economics, University of Calgary; "Labour Shortages in Saskatchewan," School of Public Policy, University of Calgary, SPP Research Papers, Volume 6, Issue 4, January 2013. http://www.policyschool.ucalgary.ca/sites/default/files/research/emerysasklabour-online.pdf

Employment and Development Canada, Snapshot of Racialized Poverty in Canada. Accessed at http://www.esdc.gc.ca/eng/communities/reports/poverty_profile/snapshot.shtml, http://cjrs-rcsr.org/archives/20-1-2/Halli-Kazemipur.pdf

Errington, Jane. "Ladies and School Mistresses, Educating Women in Early Nineteenth Century Upper, Canada," *Historical Studies in Education*.

Evans, Pete. "Less than Half of Canadians with Disabilities have jobs." Statscan, Evans, Pete, CBC News Dec 03, 2014 12:59 PM ET http://www.cbc.ca/news/business/less-than-half-of-canadian-adults-with-disabilities-have-jobs-statscan-1.2858954

Ferenc, Leslie. "Canada Failing Homeless Youth, Report Charges, *Toronto Star*, March 3, 2014, Accessed Via, York University http://yfile.news.yorku.ca/2014/03/03/canadas-under-35s-are-also-rans-in-the-wealth-race/

Fergus News Record, 17 June 1897; 20 April 1882.

Ferguson, Michael, Auditor General of Canada. 2014 Fall Report of the Auditor General of Canada, Auditor General's Opening Statement, 2014 Fall Report Press Conference.

Fleury, Michelle. "Obama's plans to make US companies pay staff overtime," Michelle Fleury reports from New York. BBC News, 13 March 2014 Last updated at 12:28 GMT, Accessed 12:59 PM MST 16/03/2014) http://www.bbc.com/news/business-26560262.

Food Banks Canada. News Release. "All Food Fit Food Banks Canada Statement on the Types of Food Distributed by Food Banks." 21 August 2014. http://www.foodbankscanada.ca/Media/News-Releases/All-Foods-Fit-Food-Banks-Canada-Statement-on-the-T.aspx

Food Banks Canada Hunger Count 2014. http://www.foodbankscanada.ca/getmedia/7739cdff-72d5-4cee-85e9-54d456669564/HungerCount_2014_EN.pdf.aspx?ext=.pdf

Forget, Evelyn L. "The Town With No Poverty, Using Health Administration Data to Revisit Outcomes of a Canadian Guaranteed Annual Income Field Experiment" The University of Manitoba, February 2011. Accessed at http://public.econ.duke.edu/~erw/197/forget-cea%20(2).pdf

Franklin, Michael. "City of Calgary to Close Midfield Mobile Home Park." CTV Calgary Published Tuesday, May 27, 2014 http://calgary.ctvnews.ca/city-of-calgary-to-close-midfield-mobile-home-park-1.1840292

Galabuzi, Grace Edward, associate professor Department of Politics and Public Administration, Ryerson University; Amy Casipullai, senior policy and communications coordinator, Ontario Council of Agencies Serving Immigrants; and Avvy Go, director, Metro Toronto Chinese & Southeast Asian Legal Clinic. "Editorial Opinion, The persistence of racial inequality in Canada," *Toronto Star*, 20 March 2012, Accessed at http://www.thestar.com/opinion/editorialopinion/2012/03/20/the_persistence_of_racial_inequality_in_canada.html

Gerson, Jen. "Alberta's $21 M media strategy employs scores more staff than actual reporters covering government." *National Post*. 03 April 2014. Accessed: http://news.nationalpost.com/2014/04/03/alberta-spends-21m-per-year-on-communications-staff-employs-many-more-people-than-reporters-covering-government/

Gilmor, Don. "Baby Boomers and Suicide, the Surprising Trend," *The Star*, Don Gillmor Special to the *Star*, Published on Fri Feb 08 2013, Accessed at http://www.thestar.com/news/insight/2013/02/08/baby_boomers_and_suicide_the_surprising_trend.html

Gladwell, Macolm. *David and Goliath, Underdogs, Misfits, and the Art of Battling Giants*. New York, Boston, London: Little, Brown and Company, 2013.

Global Voices Online. "Global Demand for Quinoa Takes Toll on Andean Farmers and Consumers," 6 November 2013. Accessed: http://globalvoicesonline.org/2013/11/06/global-demand-for-quinoa-takes-toll-on-andean-farmers-and-consumers/

Government of Canada. Poverty Profile Snapshot. http://www.esdc.gc.ca/eng/communities/reports/poverty_profile/snapshot.shtml

Gross, Dominique M. C.D. Howe Institute, "Temporary Foreign Workers in Canada: Are they really filling labour shortages?" Commentary No. 407 April 2014, Economic Growth and Innovation Accessed: http://www.cdhowe.org/pdf/commentary_407.pdf

Harper, Marjory. "The Scots in Canada," Marjory Harper, "Exiles or Entrepreneurs? Snapshots of the Scots in Canada," Chapter Two in *A Kingdom of the Mind*.

Harrison, Phyllis J. Editor, *The Home Children, Their Personal Stories*, J. Gordon Shillingford Publishing Inc., Winnipeg, 1979, 2003.

Helin, Calvin. *Dances with Dependency, Out of Poverty through Self Reliance*. Wood Hills, California: Raven Crest Publishing, 2006, 2008.

_____. *The Economic Dependency Trap*. St. Louis, Missouri, Raven Crest Publishing, 2011.

Historical Atlas of the County of Wellington, Ontario. Toronto: Historical Atlas Publishing Co., 1906.

Homeless woman fined for building her own home, CBC News, Fri, 7 Nov, 2014. https://ca.news.yahoo.com/homeless-woman-fined-building-her-110000301.html

The Homeless Hub. "Medicine Hat Plan to End Homelessness," January Update. January 2014. http://www.homelesshub.ca/resource/home-medicine-hat-our-plan-end-homelessness-january-2014-update

The Honourable Peter Talbot, Biography, Parliament of Canada, http://www.parl.gc.ca/parlinfo/Files/Parliamentarian.aspx?Item=5d49925f-1776-4eff-abc7-194cd20682a1&Language=E&Section=ALL

Hopper, Elizabeth K., Ellen L. Bassuk, and Jeffrey Olivet. "Shelter from the Storm: Trauma-Informed Care in Homelessness Services Settings," *The Open Health Services and Policy Journal*, 2009, 2, 131–151.

Ibrahim, Mariam. "Boost Alberta Legal Aid or face 'potentially devastating' consequences, CEO says" *Edmonton Journal*, 17 June 2014. http://www.edmontonjournal.com/touch/story.html?id=9944389

Ikram, Salima."The Afterlife in Ancient Egypt." Nova. 01,03,2006, http://www.pbs.org/wgbh/nova/ancient/afterlife-ancient-egypt.html

"Insurers Demand Government Change One Year After Alberta's Floods," Business News Network, 20 June 2014, http://www.bnn.ca/News/2014/6/20/Insurers-demand-government-change-one-year-after-Albertas-floods.aspx.

Ivison, John. "With Foreign Worker Changes, Jason Kenney Has Done a Great Deal to Insulate Himself," *National Post*, 20 June 2014. http://fullcomment.nationalpost.com/2014/06/20/john-ivison-with-the-temporary-foreign-worker-changes-jason-kenney-has-done-a-great-deal-to-insulate-himself/

Kaszlus, Jeremy. "If you were disturbed by the anti-homeless spikes in London, Consider Calgary." Urban Compass Calgary, *Metro News*, 7 July 2014, Accessed at http://metronews.ca/voices/urban-compass-calgary/1088113/if-you-were-disturbed-by-the-anti-homeless-spikes-in-london-consider-calgary/

Kitteringham, E. "Where is Albertans' compassion for less fortunate?", Letter to the Editor on July 13, 2014, *Lethbridge Herald*, http://lethbridgeherald.com/commentary/letters-to-the-editor/2014/07/13/where-is-albertans-compassion-for-less-fortunate/

Krishnan, Manisha. "Homeless Artists Transform East Village CrackWall, *Calgary Herald*," http://www.calgaryherald.com/news/calgary/Homeless+artists+transform+East+Village+crack+wall/9889669/story.html

Kwan, Amanda. "Toronto's affordable housing shortage sparks growth of illegal suburban rooming houses," *The Globe and Mail*, Friday, Oct. 17 2014, http://www.theglobeandmail.com/news/toronto/torontos-affordable-housing-shortage-sparks-growth-of-illegal-suburban-rooming-houses/article21153160/

"Last Resort for the Poor: The Almshouse,1843–1900," from "The New Brunswick Reader" (Saturday insert to the *Telegraph-Journal*) 14 September, 2002 copied with permission at PoorhouseStory.com, http://www.poorhousestory.com/CANADA_Article_Whalen.htm

Leo, Geoff. "Advice to Saskatchewan firm 'intimidating' to foreign workers, law prof says email about 'Canadianized' employees not a threat, owner insists," CBC News Posted: May 05, 2014 5:30 AM CT Last Updated: May 05, 2014 8:44 AM CT http://www.cbc.ca/news/canada/saskatchewan/advice-to-saskatchewan-firm-intimidating-to-foreign-workers-law-prof-says-1.2628486

Leslie, Keith. Ontario NDP PCs Blast Money Mart's 50% cash for gift card fee. CTV News. December 4, 2014.http://www.ctvnews.ca/politics/ont-ndp-pc-blast-money-mart-s-50-cash-for-gift-card-fee-1.2133206#ixzz3LekxuaU6

Lethbridge Herald. "Destitute," 23 December 1936, p. 7. Accessed at *Lethbridge Herald* Digital Archives, University of Lethbridge Newspaper Archives, http://universityoflethbridge.newspaperarchive.com.proxy.lethlib.ca/lethbridge-herald/1936-12-23/page-7/?tag=destitute&rtserp=tags/destitute?pd=23&pm=12&py=1936

Letourneau, Nicole and Justin Joschko. "Good Parenting key to breaking the cycle of poverty," *Toronto Star*, 26 October 2013, Accessed at http://www.thestar.com/opinion/commentary/2013/10/26/good_parenting_key_to_breaking_cycle_of_poverty.html.

Levitz, Stephanie. "$46 per Canadian a year could drastically reduce homelessness: report, October 29, 2014." The Canadian Press. Accessed at CTV News: http://www.ctvnews.ca/canada/46-per-canadian-a-year-could-drastically-reduce-homelessness-report-1.2076556.

Lunn, Susan. "WWI soldiers' files being digitized by Library and Archives Canada Archives begins painstaking process of getting its most-requested items online" CBC News Posted: Dec 25, 2014 9:00 PM ET Last Updated: Dec 25, 2014 9:00 PM ET.

Lye, Chandra."Alberta health minister surprised after PC Party delegates vote in favour of health care premiums," CTV Edmonton,November 24, 2013 Accessed: http://edmonton.ctvnews.ca/alberta-health-minister-surprised-after-pc-party-delegates-vote-in-favour-of-health-care-premiums-1.1558420#ixzz3N8g3V6IS

McDaniel, Susan, Bonnie Watt-Malcolm, and Lloyd Wong."Is the math Sufficient? Aging Workforce and the Future Labour Market in Canada," pp. 1–19, Prentice Institute, University of Lethbridge. Dec 15, 2013. http://www.uleth.ca/prenticeinstitute/sites/prenticeinstitute/files/KnowledgeSynthesis%20full%20report%20--McDaniel%20Watt-Malcolm%20Wong.pdf

McGee, Thomas D. "Am I remembered in Erin?" accessed at From-Ireland.net http://www.from-ireland.net/poem/am-i-remembered-in-erin/

Macionis, John J. and Linda Gerber. *Sociology*, Sixth Canadian Edition, Pearson, London, New York, Accessed at http://wps.pearsoned.ca/ca_ph_macionis_sociology_6/73/18923/4844438.cw/index.html 19 March, 2014.

Make Something Edmonton.ca details plans for Edmontons's 1st River Valley Food Forest: http://www.makesomethingedmonton.ca/projects/506-edmontons-1st-river-valley-food-forest/

Mas, Susana. "Temporary foreign worker overhaul imposes limits, hikes inspections Cap on low-wage temporary workers to be phased in over 2 years," CBC News Posted: Jun 20, 2014 1:10 PM ET Last Updated: Jun 20, 2014 10:46 PM ET http://www.cbc.ca/news/politics/temporary-foreign-worker-overhaul-imposes-limits-hikes-inspections-1.2682209

Mascarelli, Amanda. "Social isolation shortens lifespan, Ageing study finds being alone is a health risk," *Nature*, 25 March 2013 Accessed: http://www.nature.com/news/social-isolation-shortens-lifespan-1.12673

"More than 230,000 Ontario adults contemplated suicide last year: CAMH," The Canadian Press, CTV News December 4, 2014 6:07AM EST Accessed: http://www.ctvnews.ca/health/more-than-230-000-ontario-adults-contemplated-suicide-last-year-camh-1.2132224#ixzz3Kxp7Feny

Morris, Marika and updated by Tahira Gonsalves. *Women and Poverty—Third Edition*, Canadian Research Institute for the Advancement of Women, Accessed at http://criaw-icref.ca/WomenAndPoverty, 5:45 19:03 2014

Mullainathan, Sendhil and Eldar Shafir. *In Scarcity: Why Having Too Little Means So Much*. Times Books.

Murphy, Barbara. *On the Street, How We Created the Homeless*, Winnipeg" J. Gordon Shillingford Publishing Inc. 2000.

_____. *The Ugly Canadian, The Rise and Fall of a Caring Society*, J. Gordon Shillingford Publishing, Inc., 1999.

National Public Radio. "Increasing Court Fees Punish the Poor," 19 05 2014. http://www.npr.org/2014/05/19/312158516/increasing-court-fees-punish-the-poor.

Niven, Frederick. *A Kingdom of the Mind: How the Scots Helped Make Canada*, Peter E. Rider and Heather McNabb, editors. Montreal, Quebec, McGill-Queen's University Press, 2006.

Palmer, Bryan D. and Gaétan Heroux. "Cracking the Stone: The Long History of Capitalist Crisis and Toronto's Dispossessed,1830–1930", *Labour / Le Travail*, Athabasca University Press, accessed via http://content.ebscohost.com.proxy.chinookarch.ab.ca/pdf27_28/pdf/2012/7JI/01May12/79363469.pdf?T=P&P=AN&K=79363469&S=R&D=afh&EbscoContent=dGJyMNLr4oSeqLI4yOvsOLCmroyep7JSr6i4SrWWxWXS&ContentCustomer=dGJyMPGnsEyyr7FIuePfgeyx44Dt6fIA

Payton, Laura. Temporary Foreign Worker Program faces renewed call for audit CBC News Posted: 05 May 2014 http://www.cbc.ca/news/politics/temporary-foreign-worker-program-faces-renewed-call-for-audit-1.2632231.

Peel, Bruce, revised by Auguste Vachon. "Emblems of Canada," *The Canadian Encyclopedia*, Historica Canada, 04 October 2011, Last Edited 16 December 2014. http://www.thecanadianencyclopedia.ca/en/article/emblems-of-canada/

Platt, Michael. "Inappropriate behaviour forces closure of public self-cleaning toilets in East Village," *Calgary Sun*, 06 May 2014. Accessed at http://www.calgarysun.com/2014/05/06/inappropriate-behaviour-forces-closure-of-public-self-cleaning-toilets-in-east-village.

"Poor House and Hospital," *Fergus Lightning Express*, 15 March 1872, p. 2 courtesy of the Wellington County Museum and Archives.

"The psychology of scarcity, days late, dollars short, those with too little have a lot on their mind," *The Economist*, Aug 31st 2013, From the print edition, Accessed: http://www.economist.com/news/books-and-arts/21584303-those-too-little-have-lot-their-mind-days-late-dollars-short

Pyke, Alan. "Impoverished Mother Dies in Jail Cell Over Unpaid Fines For Her Kids Missing School." 12 June 2014 http://thinkprogress.org/economy/2014/06/12/3448105/mother-dies-jail-cell-fines/

Rechavi, Oded, Leah Houri-Ze'evi, Sarit Anava, Wee Siong Sho Goh, Sze Yen Kerk, Gregory J. Hannon, Oliver Hobert, "Starved worms lived longer. Starvation-Induced Transgenerational Inheritance of Small RNAs in C. elegans,"*Cell*, 08 August 2014, Accessed at 4:15 PM http://dx.doi.org/10.1016/j.cell.2014.06.020

Rodriguez, Tori. "Writing Can Help Injuries Heal," *Scientific American*, 17 October 2013.

Roman, Nan and Lisa Stand. *The Homeless Hub*, Spring 2012. http://www.homelesshub.ca/resource/housing-first HOME » http://www.shelterforce.org/article/2755/housing_first/

Rogers, Jaime and Alina Turner. "Medicine Hat Will Become Canada's First Community to End Homelessness." *The Homeless Hub*, May 15, 2014 http://www.homelesshub.ca/blog/2015-medicine-hat-will-become-canadas-first-community-end-homelessness.

Rourke, Tim. "The Manitoba Mincome Study; Even a small Guaranteed Income has dramatic positive effects on society," Citizen's Income, Toronto, Oct. 2009 Accessed at http://www.livableincome.org/atrmincome.htm

Saul, Nick. Newsletter, Community Food Centres Canada, "Good Food is just the beginning," 29 December 2014.

Senate of Canada. "In From the Margins, Part II: Reducing Barriers to Social Inclusion and Social Cohesion," Report of the Standing Senate Committee on Social Affairs, Science and Technology, The Honourable Kelvin K. Ogilvie, Chair, The Honourable Art Eggleton, P.C., Deputy Chair, June 2013.

Shaw, Matthew. *Great Scots!: How the Scots Created Canada*. Heartland Associates, Winnipeg: 2003.

Shingler, Benjamin. "Guaranteed Annual Income Proposed. $20,000 per person: Activists push for guaranteed minimum income for Canadians," The Canadian Press, Sunday, June 29th, 2014.

Skelton, Oscar Douglas. *Life and Time of Sir Alexander Tilloch Galt*. Toronto: Oxford University Press, 1920

"Social Agencies Worry Over Fate of Midfield residents," *Calgary Herald*. http://www.calgaryherald.com/news/calgary/Social+agencies+worry+fate+Midfield+residents/9886607/story.html

Social Housing in Action. "Bringing Lethbridge Home," 2013 Homeless Census Report, Prepared for Social Housing in Action by: The Community and Social Development Group, City of Lethbridge with assistance from: Jerry Firth, Practicum Student, Faculty of Social Work University of Calgary Southern Alberta Region, November 2013, Accessed at http://www.bringinglethbridgehome.ca/sites/default/files/Bringing%20Lethbridge%20Home%20-%20Homeless%20Census%20Report%202013.pdf.

Stevens, Harvey. *A Proposal for Reforming Social Security for Non-Elderly Adults in Canada*, Basic Income Canada, Winnipeg, March 2014.

Tenneriello, Tina. Morning Reporter, CJAD News. "http://www.cjad.com/cjad-news/2014/06/10/spikes-to-keep-homeless-people-away-from-businesses "Spikes to keep homeless people away from businesses." Posted on 6/10/2014 10:36:00 AM http://www.cjad.com/cjad-news/2014/06/10/spikes-to-keep-homeless-people-away-from-businesses

Thia, James. "Prince Albert woman assaulted, burned to the bone, Marlene Bird to have second leg amputation after extensive burns to body," 13 June 2014 8:00am | Last Updated: June 13, 2014 11:22amhttp://cjme.com/story/prince-albert-woman-assaulted-burned-bone/366937

Thomson, Aly. "'Extremely low' number of people with disabilities in politics, professor says," The Canadian Press. July 19th 2014. http://www.thecanadianpress.com/english/online/OnlineFullStory.aspx?filename=DOR-MNNCP.2728ee57e0284876aa4b21fd0bbb21a4.CPKEY2008111303&newsitemid=29191009&languageid=1

Tomlinson, Kathy. "CBC News Bank apologizes, cancels fee after Go Public takes on Story," CBC News, Jun 24, 2014. http://www.cbc.ca/news/canada/ottawa/scotiabank-hit-injured-soldier-with-7k-mortgage-penalty-1.2684694

Tough, Paul. "The Poverty Clinic, Can a Stressful Childhood Make You Sick?" *The New Yorker*, March 21, 2011, Paul Tough, http://www.newyorker.com/magazine/2011/03/21/the-poverty-clinic

Tuttle, Brad. "Foreclosures, House Flipping is Hot Again,"16 October 2012 http://business.time.com/2012/10/16/house-flipping-is-hot-again/

Tyler, Tracey, Legal Affairs Reporter. "When 'poorhouse' wasn't only an expression," *Toronto Star*, 03 January 2009, Accessed March 15, 6:45 PM at http://www.thestar.com/news/2009/01/03/when_poorhouse_wasnt_only_an_expression.html

Van Rassell, Jason. "Banff Meeting Offers Minister Opportunity to Press Ottawa for Legal Aid Funding," *Calgary Herald*, 29 October 2014. http://www.calgaryherald.com/news/Banff+meeting+offers+ministers+opportunity+press+Ottawa+legal+funding/10292916/story.html

Vancouver Sun. Squatters face eviction from Crown land/It has taken Tony Smith two years to build his cabin, August 26, 2009. http://www.canada.com/story.html?id=c48b468d-e452-4480-9255-5e88e9e35be3#__federated=1

Wainwright, Oliver. "Poor Doors not the worst thing about social housing." *The Guardian*. 30 July 2014. Accessed at http://www.theguardian.com/artanddesign/architecture-design-blog/2014/jul/30/poor-door-social-housing-apartheid

Waegemakers Schiff, Jeanette, Ph.D., and Alina Turner, Ph.D. Alberta Rural Homelessness Report, Turner Research & Strategy Inc., June 2014, downloaded from Alberta Centre for Child, Family, and Community Research & University of Calgary, faculty of social work, 16 May 2014 Accessed at http://www.ardn.ca/programs/rural-remote-homelessness-2013/.

"Wealthiest 1% Earn 10 Times More than Average Canadian, Canada's rich earn on average $381,300 a year and are mostly male, white and married," The Canadian Press, CBC.ca, Business, Tax Season, http://www.cbc.ca/news/business/wealthiest-1-earn-10-times-more-than-average-canadian-1.170301719 March 2014.

Whalen, James M. "Last Resort for the Poor 1843–1900," *New Brunswick Reader*, Insert into the *Telegraph Journal*, St. John, NB. September 14, 2002, Accessed on Poorhouse Story.com.

Willets, Philippa. "March of the Food Snobs," Disability Intersections, 22 January 2014. Accessed: http://disabilityintersections.com/2014/01/march-of-the-food-snobs/.

"Woman's Legs Amputated after she was beaten, burned," The Canadian Press, CTV Saskatoon, 13 June 2014 6:52AM CST. Accessed at http://saskatoon.ctvnews.ca/prince-albert-woman-s-legs-amputated-after-she-was-beaten-burned-1.1866997#ixzz3NMqhAUPL

"Woolner," *Biographical History of Waterloo*, pp. 685–689. Accessed at http://ebybook.region.waterloo.on.ca/ebybrowser.php?volume=2&page=685.

Youngblut, Shelley. "What will make the housing boom go bust? 'Greed'," *The Globe and Mail*, 14 April 2012. http://www.theglobeandmail.com/life/home-and-garden/real-estate/what-will-make-the-housing-boom-go-bust-greed/article4100579/?page=all

Zentner, Caroline. "Minimum Wage is not Enough, Lethbridge has the second highest number of low-wage workers among Alta. cities," *Lethbridge Herald*, 31 August 2013.

Websites

About.com. German Language. "Barbara, The Name and Legend." http://german.about.com/library/blbarbara.htm

Alberta Centre for Sustainable Rural Communities, A joint initiative of the University of Alberta—Augustana Campus and the Faculty of Agricultural, Life and Environmental Sciences. http://www.augustana.ualberta.ca/research/centres/acsrc/

Alberta Civil Liberties Research Centre. "What is Access to Justice, Five Different Views?" Accessed at http://www.aclrc.com/what-is-access-to-justice/ 20 December 2014.

Archives Association of Ontario, Guelph Public Library Archives, City of Guelph Fonds, Accessed at Archeion, http://www.archeion.ca/city-of-guelph-fonds;rad,16 March 2014, 6:55 pm.

Basic Income Canada. "The Fourteenth Annual North American Basic Income Guarantee Congress," Biencanada.ca Accessed at http://biencanada.ca/news/,December 2014.

BMC Medicine: http://www.biomedcentral.com/bmcmed/

"Boucher, Margaret Ruttan (Scott)," Biography.ca http://www.biographi.ca/en/bio/boucher_margaret_ruttan_16E.html

Calgary Municpal Land Commission, East Village Master Plan http://www.calgarymlc.ca/explore-projects/east-village/master-plan.

Canadian Red Cross, "The Cycle of Poverty." PDF Accessed at http://www.redcross.ca/crc/documents/What-We-Do/Emergencies-and-Disasters-WRLD/education-resources/poverty_cycle_diagram_povdisease.pdf 4:34 19/03/2014

Canadians for Public Justice. "Poverty in Canada," http://www.cpj.ca/content/poverty-canada 29 April, 2008.

City of Lethbridge policy on family passes: http://www.lethbridge.ca/Things-To-Do/Aquatics-Pools/Pages/Aquatic-Pass-Programs.aspx

Collections Canada, "Alberta Rural Life." http://www.collectionscanada.gc.ca/eppp-archive/100/200/301/ic/can_digital_collections/pasttopresent/rural_life/index.html

Collections Canada, Love and Marriage in 19th Century Canada (wedding dress colours): http://www.collectionscanada.gc.ca/love-and-marriage/031001-5300-e.html

Community Food Centres Canada: http://cfccanada.ca/

Conference Board of Canada, How Canada Performs, International Rankings, Suicides, Accessed: http://www.conferenceboard.ca/hcp/details/society/suicides.aspx

Dalzeilbarn.com http://www.dalzielbarn.com/pages/TheFarm/BuildACabin.html

East Village Experience, http://www.evexperience.com

"Face of Poverty, Consultation, An Interfaith Coalition Working To Eliminate Poverty." Accessed 19/03/2014.

Galt Museum, "The Lethbridge Nursing Mission. http://www.galtmuseum.com/permalinkA/64467/

Manitoba Historical Society, "Scott Nursing Mission,"http://www.mhs.mb.ca/docs/sites/scottnursingmission.shtml

MargoFournierCentre: http://www.citypa.ca/Residents/Facilities/MargoFournierCentre.aspx#.U5ssTpRdWSM

Names Listed in the Towns and Villages from the 1871 Gazetter for East Garafraxa Township (Wellington County,) Accessed: http://www.rootsweb.ancestry.com/~onduffer/directories/Garafraxa/1871gazetteer.html

Ontario Plaques: http://ontarioplaques.com/Plaques/Plaque_Grey23.html

Ontario Potatoes, "About Potatoes." Accessed: http://www.ontariopotatoes.ca/about-potatoes.

Open Arms Patient Advocacy Society, http://www.openarmsadvocacy.com.

Parliament of Canada. "PRB 07-22E Poverty Reduction in Canada—The Federal Role," 2007.

Parliament of Canada. Our Parliament, An Introduction to How Parliament Works, Accessed: http://www.parl.gc.ca/about/parliament/education/ourcountryourparliament/html_booklet/democracy-defined-e.html

Plan Canada, "The cycle of poverty: What is it and how is Plan helping to break it?" Accessed: http://plancanada.ca/cycle-of-poverty 4:30 19 March 2014.

Potatogoodness.com, a potato has only 110 calories, and is high in fibre, Vitamin C, potassium, and Vitamin B6. Accessed at http://www.potatogoodness.com/nutrition/nutritional-facts/.

Povnet.org, Race and Ethnicity, http://www.povnet.org/news/issues/ethnicity-and-race Povnet.org Accessed 5:04 19 March 2014.

Public Health Agency of Canada Suicide-Related Research in Canada: A Descriptive Overview Health of Populations References, http://www.phac-aspc.gc.ca/publicat/mh-sm/suicide-research/app-x2d-eng.php.

Rootsweb.ancestry.com, Dufferin Townships, Accessed: http://www.rootsweb.ancestry.com/~onduffer/townships/fraxa.html

St. John's Cathedral, "About Our Past, Margaret Scott," http://stjohnscathedral.ca/about/our-past/cemetery/margaret-scott/

Salvation Army.ca, From Middle Class to Homelessness: How One Man Found a Path out of Destitution,Posted in Articles, Feature, Mobile by SalvationArmy.ca October 28. http://www.research4children.com/theme/common/sitemap-a-to-z.cfm Alberta Centre for Child

Saskatchewan Party. http://saskparty.com/index.php?pageid=Record

Senator Art Eggleton.ca. "Poverty Fact Sheet," in "From the Margins: A Call to End Poverty in Canada," Accessed: http://senatorarteggleton.ca/Issues/Poverty/TimetoBreaktheCycleofPoverty.aspx 4:44 19/03/2014

Social Housing Action, City of Lethbridge. Accessed March 13, 2014. http://www.socialhousing.ca/page.cfm?pgID=32

The Stop. http://thestop.org/node/68/community-gardens

Sustainable Food Edmonton. http://sustainablefoodedmonton.org/urban-ag-high/inspiring-education-through-urban-agriculture/

Toronto.ca http://www1.toronto.ca/wps/portal/contentonly?vgnextoid=2c942118b7412410VgnVCM10000071d60f89RCRD

University of Waterloo, "Young Immigrants to Canada," uwaterloo.ca Accessed: http://jubilation.uwaterloo.ca/~marj/genealogy/homeadd.html, March 15, 2014, 7:30 PM.

Wedding Dress in 1861 Photo tartan with lace wedding dress. Accessed: http://www.memorialhall.mass.edu/collection/itempage.jsp?itemid=15807&img=5&level=advanced&transcription=0

Wellington County Museum and Archives,"If These Walls Could Speak: The House of Industry and Refuge, 1877–1947," Wellington County Museum and Archives, Wellington.ca. Accessed at http://www.wellington.ca/en/discover/ifthesewallscouldspeakthehouseofindustryandrefuge.asp.

When the Middle Class Becomes Homeless—YouTube, Posted by 'Ronzig the Wizard,' https://www.youtube.com/watch?v=Dk_iiVgJi6A

Wildrose.ca http://www.wildrose.ca/caringforvulnerable
Workhouse.org http://www.workhouses.org.uk/intro/

Historical Records

Belwood W.1 Tweedsmuir History, Volume 3.

GILCHRIST, Barbara, Residence: Garrafraxa, Father: John, to Michael SMITH, Residence: Garafraxa, Father: Thos., 1861, Ref. # 1:58. Accessed: http://boards.ancestry.ca/thread.aspx?mv=flat&m=334&p=localities. northam.canada.ontario.wellington

1861 Census of Canada, Library and Archives Canada

1852 Census of Canada, Library and Archives Canada

1871 Census of Canada, Library and Archives Canada

1901 Census of Canada, Library and Archives Canada

1916 Census of Canada (Alberta and Saskatchewan) Library and Archives Canada

Homestead Record, Section 34, Township 48, Range 10, Film #2400 in Accession #1970.313 at Provincial Archives at Alberta.

SMITH, Barbara, Residence: E. Garafraxa, Father: John GILCHRIST, to William BOYLE, Residence: W. Garafraxa, Father: Thomas, 1869, Ref. # 2:20. Accessed at Gilchrist http://boards.ancestry.ca/thread. aspx?mv=flat&m=334&p=localities.northam.canada.ontario.wellington

Photos the Boyle House: University of Guelph photos. http://wcm.pastperfect-online.com/39564cgi/mweb.exe?request=record; id=3A56EB0A-4341-4AAB-9FA8-056747883064;type=301

Maps, Wills, and Land Documents accessed via the Wellington County Museum, Wellington County, Ontario including the Will of William Boyle (1897), Will of Barbara Gilchrist Boyle (1911) Probate Papers Estate of Michael Smith (1868).

ENDNOTES

1. While several children are already married, Barbara still has three unmarried teenagers living with her. The youngest is only thirteen when William Boyle dies.
2. This is probably Barbara's best dress. She likely does not wear her fancy widow's veil when she cares for her animals or when she oversees the making of meals and housework.
3. According to the Census of 1852, Barbara, her parents, and siblings arrived in Garafaxa Township approximately 1849. "Beginnings" is based on records of my great-great-great-grandparents' household in the Census of 1852, along with archival material about life in Upper Canada, Wellington County, and the household of John and Sarah Gilchrist.
4. The first cabins put up by settlers often had no windows, although log houses built a year or so later to replace them usually did. Information on building log cabins can be found at "The Farm/Build a Cabin" on Dalzeilbarn.com.
5. Barbara comes from the feminine form of the Greek word, 'barbaros' (foreign). It means foreign woman. According to legend, Saint Barbara's father, a pagan king, imprisoned her in a tower for many years. After she defied him by becoming a Christian during her imprisonment, he ordered her executed. As she was beheaded, her father was struck by lightning.
6. Lucille H. Campey, *An Unstoppable Force, the Scottish Exodus to Canada*, Natural Heritage Books, Dundurn Group, 2008. According to Campey, many Highlander settlers climbed rope ladders to get on to the ships that would take them to Canada.
7. Ibid. Campey documents the fact that many Scots wanted to leave Scotland to settle in Canada, but were held back by the cost of fares and opposition from landlords, who did not want them to leave, especially prior to the end of the Napoleonic Wars.

8   The land the Gilchrists settled on was in the Huron Tract. If they were like most settlers, they probably intended to purchase it. When John Gilchrist died, his widow and children remained in their log cabin. They appear to have been renters, although they may have owned the house and a small acreage. A neighbour, such as land developer and innkeeper Manasah Leeson, may have bought their land. John Gilchrist may not have earned enough to complete a purchase from the Canada Company, as his neighbours (Barbara's future in-laws) Thomas and Mary Ann (Warner) Smith did.

9   Barbara never learned to read or write. However, most girls went to school in Wellington County. Both girls and boys attended school in Scotland. Perhaps emigrating at age nine interfered with her education.

10 Adolphus Egerton Ryerson, editor; John George Hodgins, and Adam Crooks, assistant editors, *The Journal of Education for Upper Canada, Volumes 7–8*, Ontario Department of Education, Toronto, 1854. p. 115. This book provides a firsthand account of schooling in colonial Canada.

11 Jane Errington, "Ladies and School Mistresses, Educating Women in early 19th Century Upper Canada," *Historical Studies in Education*, Queen's University Press, 1994.

12 John Gilchrist is listed as a labourer in the 1852 Census. He may have chopped timber, worked for a neighbouring farmer, or found construction or maintenance work with a local businessman.

13 Merin was also called Sarah. Her name appears as Sarah in the 1861 census (the family are living at the same address as in 1852), on her wedding registration, and on her tombstone. The *1852 Census of Upper Canada* record is the only place it appears as Merin. Perhaps, the enumerator wrote her sister's Mary's name down twice, or he didn't understand the Gilchrists' Scots accent, or Sarah may have been using a middle name to distinguish her from her mother in the earlier census.

14 A toonie is a Canadian two-dollar coin.

15 The Mobile Urban Street Team has the unfortunate acronym of MUST. Its supporters seem oblivious to the potential allusion to anti-pauper and anti-homeless laws intended to 'force' unwanted people of the streets.

16 It wasn't that I didn't have skills, but 95% of my work had been volunteer work. I'd organized fund-raising dinners, publicity, public meetings, and implemented caucus tours throughout southern Alberta from my kitchen table for no wage. I thought that as a young full-time mother I had to work for free to pad my resume in preparation for a career. I still have the leather-bound portfolio with the legislative crest I received from the party leader for my efforts. I was also beginning a writing career, freelancing feature articles, while I cared for my kids. The poor, the disadvantaged, the young, and those who don't have 'connections' are often told to volunteer in order

to gain experience. In my experience, volunteering rarely leads to paid work. But getting a job really isn't the point of community work anyway: service to others is. Today, I only volunteer for organizations I truly want to help with no expectations in return.

17 *Canadian Oxford Dictionary*, editor Alex Bisset, Oxford University Press, Don Mills, Ontario, 2000.

18 Thomas D'Arcy McGee, "Am I Remembered in Erin?" McGee, a radical in Ireland, renounced violence in Canada. He later became a Father of Confederation, and was assassinated for his support of Canadian Confederation.

19 Frederick Niven was a Scots-Canadian novelist who lived in British Columbia, and wrote about Scottish and First Nations themes. His papers are kept at the Glenbow Museum in Calgary, Alberta. The lines, "Scotland is a place in the sun and the rain, but more than that, it is a kingdom of the mind" and " The old love of it endures, whatever reason or necessity for living elsewhere" come from his work, *Coloured Spectacles* (Collins, London, 1938). Peter E. Rider and Heather Mcnabb reference this verse in *A Kingdom of the Mind: How the Scots Helped Make Canada*, McGill-Queen's University Press, Montreal, Quebec, 2006.

20 Nellie Bowles, "Richard Branson Speaks after Virgin Galactic Tragedy," Recode.net, 1 November 2014. Bowles covers Sir Richard Branson's statement after the Virgin Galactic Crash, in which he quotes Christopher Hadfield, Canadian ex-astronaut. Accessed: http://recode.net/2014/11/01/richard-branson-speaks-after-virgin-galactic-tragedy/

21 The Gilchrists were Highlanders who arrived in Wellington County, Upper Canada between 1848–1850. According to Lucille Campey, many Wellington County Scots came from Perthshire. Others came from the Hebrides, including a group of destitute Hebrideans, who arrived in Fergus between 1847 and 1851. Many Scots living in the town of Fergus or Nichol District came from Perthshire, Bon Accord, Elmshire and Aberdeen. Another family of Gilchrists, with similar Christian names to Barbara's family, settled in the Puslinch Township, Wellington County after emigrating from Kintyre, Argyll and Butte, Scotland. See "Attractions of the Western Peninsula," *The Scottish Pioneers of Upper Canada, 1755–1855*, pp. 90–93.

22 This sister of Barbara Gilchrist is recorded as Sarah in the *1861 Census of Upper Canada*, on her 1863 marriage registration to Abraham Woolner, and on her tombstone.

23 Barbara's youngest brother, Samuel Gilchrist, was the first member of her family to be born in Canada. It is likely that Barbara Gilchrist and William Boyle's son, Samuel James Boyle (my great-grandfather), was named after Barbara's younger brother Samuel Gilchrist.

24 Lucille Campey, "The Attractions of the Western Peninsula," *The Scottish Pioneers of Upper Canada, 1755–1855*.
25 According to researcher and author, Lucille Campey, the landlords changed their estates over to sheep farming after 1770. Kelping, fishing, raising cattle, and cutting timber were traditional Highland occupations.
26 Campey, *An Unstoppable Force*, p. 46.
27 Lucille Campey, *After the Hector, The Scottish Pioneers of Nova Scotia and Cape Breton, 1773–1852*, Natural Heritage Books, Second Edition, 2007.
28 Campey, *The Scottish Exodus to Canada*. Those back home received glowing reports about the potential for growing wealthy as Canadian farmers by those emigrating in the 1820s.
29 Campey, *An Unstoppable Force*, p. 203.
30 Bernard Bailyn, *Voyagers to the West: A Passage in the Peopling of America on the Eve of the Revolution*. Knop Doubleday, 1986, p. 61.
31 George III gave American loyalists and their descendants the title United Empire Loyalists and the right to have the letters UE after their names.
32 "Woolner," *Biographical History of Waterloo*, pp. 685–689. Accessed: http://ebybook.region.waterloo.on.ca/ebybrowser.php?volume=2&page=685. This source is informative in many respects. However, some children appear to missing from this biography, including Sarah Gilchrist's husband, Abraham Woolner.
33 The Connors (Abraham Woolner's second set of in-laws) were close neighbours of my ancestors, the Gilchrists, as well as to Abraham Woolner's second family.
34 Abraham did not die as a child. He was alive and well during the 1852 Census, and records show that he married his neighbour Sarah Gilchrist in Wellington County in 1863.
35 The enumerator of the 1852 Census recorded this child as Merin, possibly to distinguish her from her mother. He may also have written down two versions of her sister's Mary's name in error. The family was still living at the same address in 1861 where Barbara's sister's name appears as Sarah. She also appears as Sarah on her 1863 wedding registration. Barbara is no longer in the house when the enumerator arrives. Her marriage must have taken place earlier in the year.
36 The gravestone of Sarah Gilchrist and her husband, Abraham Woolner in Simcoe United Church Cemetery can be accessed online at: http://geneofun.on.ca/names/photo/1584862?PHPSESSID=63e13774a6b557bb6dfe2121d0288578
37 Campey, *An Unstoppable Force*, pp. 166–167.
38 Ibid, pp. 64, 87.
39 Oscar Skelton, *The Life and Times of Sir Alexander Tilloch Galt*, Oxford University Press, Toronto, 1920.

40 Tom Cheshire, *The Explorer Gene: How Three Generations of One Family Went Higher, Deeper and Further Than Any Before*, Short Books, London, 2013.
41 Ibid.
42 Youli Yao, Alexandra M Robinson, Fabiola Zucchi, Jerrah C. Robbins, Olena Babenko, Olga Kovalchuk, Igor Kovalchuk, David M. Olson, and Gerlinde Metz, "Ancestral Exposure to Stress Epigenetically Programs Preterm Birth Risk and Adverse Maternal and Newborn Outcomes," BMC *Medicine*, August 2014. Accessed: http://www.biomedcentral.com/1741-7015/12/121
43 Oded Rechavi, Leah Houri-Ze'evi, Sarit Anava, Wee Siong Sho Goh, Sze Yen Kerk, Gregory J. Hannon, Oliver Hobert, "Starvation-Induced Transgenerational Inheritance of Small RNAs in *C. elegans*," *Cell*, July 10. 2014.
44 Amanda Mascarelli, "Social Isolation Shortens Lifespan, Ageing Study Finds Being Alone is a Health Risk,"*Nature*, 25 March 2013 Accessed: http://www.nature.com/news/social-isolation-shortens-lifespan-1.12673
45 Campey, *The Scottish Pioneers of Upper Canada, 1755–1855*, pp. 53–54.
46 Campey, *An Unstoppable Force*, pp. 193–196.
47 Campey, *The Scottish Pioneers of Upper Canada, 1755–1855*, p. 174.
48 "If these walls could speak: The House of Industry and Refuge, 1877–1947," Wellington Country Museum and Achives. Accessed: http://www.wellington.ca/en/discover/cemeteryhoi.asp#Follow%20link%20to%20the%20House%20of%20Industry%20Cemetery%20page
49 "Poverty in Canada," Citizens for Public Justice, 2008 Accessed: http://www/content/poverty-canada
50 Murphy, *On the Street*, p. 79. At the turn of the 21st century, 17% of Canadians were poor. One in seven families were poor. One in three singles were poor.
51 Ibid. p. 85.
52 Facebook Creature Sightings' group mocks Calgary homeless, CBC News, March 11, 2014. After the site was shut down by Facebook, it reappeared a few day later, under a slightly different name. It goes by the following url: https://www.facebook.com/creat.uresightings.
53 Bryan D. Palmer and Gaétan Heroux, "Cracking the Stone: The Long History of Capitalist Crisis and Toronto's Dispossessed, 1830–1930," *Labour / Le Travail*, Athabasca University Press. According to the authors, 19th-century migrant labourers overwhelmed small towns and large cities in Ontario. These unemployed men were described as "pests," "voracious monsters," "outrageously impertinent," an "irrepressible stampede" deserving of "a well-aimed dose of buckshot rubbed in well with salt-petre." They were described in newspapers as "work-shy and degenerate."

54   The Canadian Press, "Woman's legs amputated after she was beaten, burned," CTV Saskatoon, June 13, 2014. Accessed http://saskatoon.ctvnews.ca/prince-albert-woman-s-legs-amputated-after-she-was-beaten-burned-1.1866997#ixzz3NMqhAUPL

55   Oliver Wainwright, "Poor Doors: not the worst thing about social housings," *The Guardian*, Wednesday 30 July 2014. Wainwright explains that the roots of poor doors are in old-style segregation. http://www.theguardian.com/artanddesign/architecture-design-blog/2014/jul/30/poor-door-social-housing-apartheid

56   "Anti-loitering spikes removed after Montreal mayor voices outrage, Denis Coderre says metal spikes meant to deter people from sitting on sidewalk are a 'disgrace,'" CBC News, Jun 10, 2014. Accessed: http://www.cbc.ca/news/canada/montreal/anti-loitering-spikes-removed-after-montreal-mayor-voices-outrage-1.2670842

57   Tina Tenneriello, morning reporter, "Spikes to keep homeless people away from businesses," CJAD News, 10 June 2014. Accessed: http://www.cjad.com/cjad-news/2014/06/10/spikes-to-keep-homeless-people-away-from-businesses

58   Jeremy Kaszlus, "If You Were Disturbed by the Anti-homeless Spikes in London, Consider Calgary." Urban Compass Calgary, *Metro News*, 7 July 2014, Accessed: http://metronews.ca/voices/urban-compass-calgary/1088113/if-you-were-disturbed-by-the-anti-homeless-spikes-in-london-consider-calgary/

59   The Canadian Press, "More than 230,000 Ontario adults contemplated suicide last year: CAMH," CTV News, 4 December 2014, Accessed: http://www.ctvnews.ca/health/more-than-230-000-ontario-adults-contemplated-suicide-last-year-camh-1.2132224#ixzz3Kxp7Feny

60   "How Canada Performs, International Rankings, Suicides," How Canada Performs, Conference Board of Canada, Accessed at: http://www.conferenceboard.ca/hcp/details/society/suicides.aspx

61   S. Burrows, N. Auger, M. Roy, C. Alix, "Socio-economic Inequalities in Suicide Attempts and Suicide Mortality in Québec, Canada, 1990–2005," *Public Health* 124, Feb 2010, pp. 78–85.

62   Amanda Mascarelli, "Social Isolation Shortens Lifespan, Ageing Study Finds Being Alone is a Health Risk," *Nature*, 25 March 2013 Accessed at: http://www.nature.com/news/social-isolation-shortens-lifespan-1.12673

63   Amanda Kwan, "Toronto's affordable housing shortage sparks growth of illegal suburban rooming houses," *The Globe and Mail*, Friday, Oct. 17 2014. As Kwan explains, illegal rooming houses are a booming business. Sadly, renting a room in a house with people you do not know can be a dangerous practice that leaves the poor even more vulnerable to theft or

physical attack or injury through negligence. Accessed: http://www.theglobeandmail.com/news/toronto/torontos-affordable-housing-shortage-sparks-growth-of-illegal-suburban-rooming-houses/article21153160/

64 Like many do-gooders, I was afraid of the people I purported to know how to help.

65 The mall staff did call the ambulance eventually.

66 This hotel has since been torn down.

67 Although I remember cooking Christmas dinner for my kids in a toaster oven at that hotel, I rarely saw my own children during the nearly two years I lived there. The building and neighbourhood were too dangerous. On paper I had joint custody, negotiated by a mediator at the time of separation. I was supposed to have my daughter with me full-time, my teenage sons were supposed to be with me on weekends. I was supposed to be receiving child support ordered by the Court of Queen's Bench.

68 My husband seemed to rally the last month he was home, going for therapy and to a Twelve Step Program. He made the decision to sell his business and to pursue a salaried job related to his former careers in IT and management. He told me that he had secured a new job working with a chartered bank. He appeared to work on a Virtual Private Network from his home office and to attend staff meetings downtown. I have no hard evidence that this was not true, although I suspect he lost the job in the week before the assault. His downward slide in the last 48 hours started Wednesday morning, after an apparent meeting downtown, and escalated when he returned home upset after a twelve-step meeting Thursday evening. In retrospect, I believe his short rally was genuine, but that he could not sustain it or the new job, just as a terminally ill person who rallies in their last weeks may die suddenly after appearing to be getting stronger.

69 We could see two bridges—the historic railway bridge and the busier traffic bridge. It was the traffic bridge that we used to measure water because the water levels are easier to measure on cement.

70 My somewhat strange train of thought after the accident does not reflect on Lethbridge Transit or Tim Horton's staff. I am sure they would have helped me.

71 A judge released him two weeks later to await trial. He relapsed and wound up on the street within a week or two, telling people that I was dead and the dog was at the kennel. I got calls from acquaintances informing me that he was beaten up on the street, was high on something, terrified, and barely coherent. I planned his funeral after one of those calls. A street minister found him overdosed on prescription medications, sick with pneumonia, and ordered the ambulance to take him to the hospital.

72 My parents did not get my email for a couple of days. The flood knocked out telecommunications in large swaths of Alberta.

73 I remember his last ambulance ride from our home. I came home from teaching a writing class to find him passed out from drinking windshield washer fluid. He wound up in the intensive care unit on dialysis for three days before they sent him to the psychiatric ward for another two and half weeks. My heart fell to the pit of my stomach as I watched medical staff offer him 'dope' in the psychiatric ward (it was morphine) as he lined up like an addict to get his fix. I will never forget the psychiatrist's words the night before he released him, when I asked him, "Will I be seeing George and Dennis when he comes home?" (George and Dennis were my husband's imaginary friends, the ones he only saw when he took all his meds at once or spiked them with Tylenol, vodka or windshield washer fluid.) The doctor looked me in the eye and said, "I think they will disappear with time." The doctors sent my husband home on Valentine's Day. He relapsed within an hour of coming home, although he played at treatment off and on, for a few months more.

74 I got a bill from Alberta Health Services after a routine medical appointment. Alberta Health Services explained to me that my card had been cancelled when my husband or one of his 'legal or support team' requested that I be removed from our family health care card. It took me an afternoon on the phone to resolve the problem. There are no health care premiums in Alberta. So there was no monetary reason to remove me from the card without notice. Further, we were still legally married, no division of assets had occurred, and both my husband and his support team knew that I had sustained several injuries, including emotional trauma and a head injury.

75 I allowed some retirement funds to be unlocked to ensure the mortgage was paid after my injury. The intent was to pay ahead on the house for at least one year, to allow time for us to consider options that would ensure we did not lose the investment, if the house was sold. The $24,000 released represented nearly twenty-two months of taxes and mortgage payments on our house. Under Alberta's Dower Act, I was entitled to fifty percent of sale, even though my husband put our house in his name when we bought it. For some reason, the house was put into foreclosure within three months, apparently at my husband's instruction and/or his lawyer's advice. The house was then sold at a price well below the expected price. Had the money had been applied to the mortgage and the house been prepared for sale, significant financial losses could have been avoided.

76 These statements were contained in the documents read out by my attacker's criminal lawyer at his sentencing. They are in the public record.

77 I filed a complaint with the College of Physicians and Surgeons in Alberta about what I believed to be the over-prescribing of narcotics (ostensibly for an old back injury) to my husband before I was injured. I received a letter

from the College of Physicians and Surgeons in October 2013 indicating that the College had determined there indeed had been errors in treatment, and that the College was working with the general practitioner to address those issues. At sentencing, my husband was still taking most of the medications that I was concerned about. The medication list was read out in court. At that point he had overdosed at least twice at the mission where he was living— once on the day of his first trial in January 2014 and 24 hours before his sentencing hearing in July 2014. I have copies of ambulance bills that were sent to my home after those events, including the one sent to our home after he was taken from Parkside Home to the Chinook Regional Hospital in an ambulance on full life support the day before his first sentencing hearing. The judge was told by defence counsel he was doing well at the Parkside Home. Clearly, he was not.

78 Occasionally, especially in the early weeks after my injury, my daughter would bring groceries to my house. Without her help, I would have spent even more time worrying about how to manage.

79 Chloe is my dog.

80 The day after my husband agreed to plead guilty, I went to court to challenge the mortgage company's assertion that the house was overpriced. My husband's civil lawyer was there, too. He told the judge his client, who already knew he was heading to jail, was thinking of taking possession of the house.

81 Kelly Cryderman, "Almost a year after the Alberta flood, housing market yet to recover," *The Globe and Mail*, Apr. 27 2014. Accessed: http://www.theglobeandmail.com/report-on-business/economy/housing/after-the-flood-the-deluge/article18293150/. Some financial institutions gave Alberta mortgage holders an amnesty after the flood. For example, First National Financial LP extended a three- to six-month mortgage amnesty to dozens of Alberta customers following the floods.

82 The Breeze Card is the pre-loaded electronic fare card riders use to pay fares on Lethbridge Transit http://www.lethbridge.ca/living-here/getting-around/Transit/Pages/electronic-fare-card.aspx

83 Taken from my personal notes.

84 Tori Rodriguez, "Writing Can Help Injuries Heal," *Scientific American*, 17 October 2013. As this article points out, writing has both physical and emotional benefits for patients recovering from brain injury and trauma.

85 "Love and Marriage in 19th Century Canada (wedding dress colours)" Collections Canada, Accessed: http://www.collectionscanada.gc.ca/love-and-marriage/031001-5300-e.html and "Wedding Dress in 1861," Photo of tartan with lace wedding dress, Memorial Hall Museum Online. Accessed: http://www.memorialhall.mass.edu/collection/itempage.jsp?itemid=15807&img=5&level=advanced&transcription=0

86 Sarah was also called Merin.
87 Victorians were fascinated with Egyptian mummies. They had mummy unwrapping parties. Source: Salima Ikram, "The Afterlife in Ancient Egypt," *Nova*. 3 January 2006. Accessed: http://www.pbs.org/wgbh/nova/ancient/afterlife-ancient-egypt.html
88 This was a house wedding, according to the marriage record.
89 The Gilchrists were Church of Scotland (Presbyterian) Highlanders according to both the 1852 Census of Canada and 1861 Census of Canada.
90 I found no tombstone or death notices recorded for John Gilchrist during my research. Nor did the archivists at Wellington County Museum and Archives.
91 Steven J. Brown and Krista A. Taylor, "Reading," *East Garafraxa, A History*, The Corporation of the Township of East Garafraxa, 2006.
92 Many Scots emigrated to areas where other family members had settled. They preferred the word emigrate (to leave a place), to the word immigrate (to move to a place) to describe their movement from one part of the empire to the other.
93 Phyllis Harrison, editor, *The Home Children, Their Personal Stories*, Winnipeg: J. Gordon Shillingford, 1979, 2003, p. 27.
94 While most records suggest they came from Leicestershire, some records say Derbyshire. At least one document speculates that Thomas and Mary Smith left a married daughter in Wales when they emigrated.
95 Thomas and Mary Smith bought their farm from the Canada Company.
96 The Smith children living with their mother, Barbara Gilchrist Smith Boyle, and William Boyle are listed as Rebecca 9, Sarah 7, William 5, and Mary 3, in 1871. This means Mary was born in 1868. She was either not yet born or a newborn when her father, Michael Smith, died.
97 Cambridge Advanced Learners Dictionary & Thesaurus, Cambridge University Press Accessed: http://dictionary.cambridge.org/dictionary/british/talk-through-your-hat. According to this dictionary, 'talk through your hat' means to "talk about something without understanding what you are talking about."
98 Thomas and Mary Warner Smith also had a son named Richard. He married Ellen Wray. Their daughter, Mary Ann Smith, married Samuel Boyle (son of Barbara Gilchrist and William Boyle). Samuel and Mary Ann Boyle are my mother's paternal grandparents. Therefore, my great-grandfather Samuel's half siblings (Rebecca, Sarah, William, and Mary Smith) were my great-grandmother Mary Ann's first cousins. In other words, Thomas and Mary Warner Smith are my great-great-great-grandparents through their son Richard and the descendants of Michael Smith are also my blood relatives—albeit distant cousins.

99 Thomas Smith lives to be 97. While at least one local history indicates that Thomas Smith ran his son Michael's farm after the young man died intestate, this must have been short-lived. The land became part of William James Boyle's estate at some point. William James Boyle left the Smith property to his step-son, William Smith (son of Barbara Gilchrist Boyle and her first husband, Michael Smith) in 1897.

101 Census records say that Barbara could read, but she signed both her own will and Michael Smith probate documents with an X. Perhaps, shame kept her from sharing this information with the enumerators. It is possible that other members of her family were also unable to read and write, but kept the information from the enumerator out of shame.

101 The Boyles, Smiths, and Gilchrists lived in the Garafraxa District of Wellington County. Some members of the family also had farms in nearby Dufferin county.

102 William Boyle appears to have been fairly well educated. Judging from the instructions in his will, he had sound knowledge of annuities and savings. During his lifetime he was asked to run for a seat on the Township Council several times. He always refused.

103 In 1861, the Gilchrists are listed as Church of Scotland. William and Maria Boyle are listed as United Methodist. When I started my research, I believed that William Boyle was always a Congregationalist, but the records indicate that William and Barbara joined the Congregational Church after their marriage.

104 *Fergus News Record,* 17 June 1897. Some Census records are not consistent with these dates, but this article agrees with both the Historical Atlas of Wellington County and Wiliam Boyle's tombstone.

105 The Census listed ages for William and Maria Boyle's children's 1861 birthdays are Charles 6, Mary Jane 5, and Thomas 2.

106 Robert was dragged to death at age 12 by a two-year-old colt. The younger brother who witnessed the tragedy was probably my great-grandfather. Family oral history says that Samuel, then about 10 years old, scared the horse and caused his brother's death. Apparently, he talked about this incident with his children and grandchildren, as my mother's older siblings already knew the story—that it was their grandfather who had caused the horse to bolt—before I showed them the newspaper record of it. This trauma may have been behind Samuel's inability to manage the farm his father left him, and may have been the root of a life-long drinking problem. He may not have believed he deserved his inheritance.

107 Samuel James Boyle and Mary Ann Smith Boyle brought their younger children to Alberta at the end of World War 1. Two of their sons were already in Alberta. My grandfather was homesteading. His younger brother

William was a resident of Minburn, Alberta when he joined the Canadian Expeditionary Service. One daughter was married and remained with her family in Guelph, Ontario.

108 Adam married Jennie Duffield. The Duffields were a prominent Anglo-Irish family. The upwardly mobile Adam built a two-storey red brick house across the road from the original homestead that his brother Alfred inherited. Jennie and Adam employed several domestic servants and their home is described as a mansion in the 1906 Historical Atlas of Wellington County. (It was a large house, but not a mansion in any 21st-century sense.) Norman Boyle, my grandfather, worked for his uncle Adam as a teenager. He is listed as a servant in the 1911 Census, not a family member, and this may explain why he left, apparently to work as a lumberjack in the Manitoulin Islands before heading to Alberta. By that time, Samuel's drinking, gambling and bad business sense was an embarrassment to his upwardly mobile brothers Adam and Alfred. In addition, it appears that his siblings had to lend financial support to keep Samuel and Mary Ann's large family.

109 Alfred inherited the stone house William Boyle built for his family in 1882. His mother was still listed as a resident in the house in 1911, although she died that December at her daughter Sophia Talbot's house in Guelph. Alfred and his family moved to Saskatchewan in the 1930s. Together with Adam, Alfred owned a section of land in the Northwest (the ranch was in Saskatchewan) before 1906. They also owned town lots in Fergus, according to the 1906 Historical Atlas of Wellington County.

110 Pronounced Soph-I-a not Soph-ee-a.

111 Samuel was my great-grandfather.

112 Samuel married Mary Ann Smith, the daughter of Richard Smith (son of Thomas and Mary Ann Warner Smith), and Ellen Falls Smith (daughter of William Falls, and his wife, Ellen Wray). William Falls was an Enniskillin Dragoon, who received a land grant and medal after he was wounded at the Battle of Waterloo. Family oral history indicates this marriage was not popular with Barbara and William, given that Mary Ann Smith was the niece of Barbara's first husband, Michael, and first cousin of her Aunt Barbara's first set of children. It seems probable that Barbara and William were not pleased at having such a close relationship with Barbara's former in-laws.

113 Barbara and William Boyle attend the Congregational Church after their marriage, but William and Maria Kennedy Boyle are listed as United Methodist in the 1861 Census.

114 When John Gilchrist died, Sarah had five children to support in colonial Canada. Barbara found herself in an equally desperate situation when Michael Smith died without a will, leaving her to pay his debts and care for their four children, including a newborn.

115 The cow's offspring could be sold or used to build a herd. The milk, butter, cream and cheese could also be sold or used at home.
116 Some of the land had already been distributed to William's married sons. He appears to have given my great-grandparents a farm as a wedding present.
117 Census of Canada, 1911, Accessed: http://automatedgenealogy.com/census11/SplitView.jsp?id=51652
118 The Honourable Peter Talbot, Biography, Parliament of Canada, Accessed http://www.parl.gc.ca/parlinfo/Files/Parliamentarian.aspx?Item=5d49925f-1776-4eff-abc7-194cd20682a1&Language=E&Section=ALL
119 "If these walls could speak," Wellington County Museum and Archives.
120 "Poor House and Hospital" *Fergus Lightning Express,* 15 March 1872, p. 2.
121 "Castle gives up swastika secret," *The Scotsman,* 9 August 2008. Swastika symbols can also be found at Edinburgh Castle. The swastikas are easily seen in photos of William and Barbara's home taken when the house was 100 years old. Those photos are now in the Wellington County Museum Collection. The Boyles would be mortified to know that the ancient symbol of peace and good fortune they carved on their home, along with Christian Crosses, is now associated with hatred and genocide.
122 Wording used in Canadian wills, including that of William Boyle, to bestow property on an heir.
123 William Smith, son of Michael Smith and Barbara Gilchrist Smith Boyle, is not forgotten in William Boyle's will. Nor are his daughters and stepdaughters.
124 The girls receive money in their father's will as does his son Thomas Boyle.
125 Lucille H. Campey, *The Scottish Pioneers of Upper Canada,* p. 96. Ontarians, especially those with Scots heritage, headed to the prairies beginning in the 1870s and 1880s.
126 Industrialization in Toronto began in the 1850s, after the arrival of the railroad. By the 1870s, grey smog could be seen on the city skyline. The fledgling metropolis relied on workers from rural Canada and new immigrants keep its factories staffed. Source: Toronto.ca. Accessed: http://www1.toronto.ca/wps/portal/contentonly?vgnextoid=2c9421118b7412410vgnVCM10000071d60f89RCRD
127 In the mid-twentieth century, the poor were often elderly people. By 1947, Wellington County's House of Refuge was renamed Wellington County Home for the Aged. The Home for the Aged closed in 1972. In 1975, the Wellington Country Museum and archives opened at the same location.
128 "About Us," 'Wellington County Museum and Archives. Accessed: http://www.wellington.ca/en/discover/aboutus_museum.asp

129 Photos of William Boyle's house a century after it was built, but before it was repaired in the 1970s. Accessed: http://wcm.pastperfect-online.com/39564cgi/mweb.exe?request=record;id=3A56EB0A-4341-4AAB-9FA8-056747883064;type=301

130 By 1903, the province required every county in Ontario to have a house of refuge.

131 James M. Whalen, "Last Resort for the Poor 1843–1900," *New Brunswick Reader*, Insert into the *Telegraph Journal*, Saint John. September 14, 2002, accessed at Poorhouse Story.com. Prior to the advent of the poorhouse, Ontario's poor often wound up in jail for a night or two. Paupers faced even worse treatment in pre-Confederation New Brunswick. In the late 18th and early 19th century, prior to establishing poorhouses there, New Brunswick's poor were sold into indentured labour at auction.

132 Residents of the poorhouse were called inmates, just as people incarcerated in prison are in the 21st century. This does not necessarily mean that Canadian poorhouses were meant to punish. All residents of dwellings, including private homes, were referred to as 'inmates' in census records.

133 Men and women had separate dormitories.

134 A stone washhouse erected in 1877 to serve as a laundry, woodshed and "dead house." A dead house was a building "to place deceased inmates before they were buried on the grounds." The poorhouse also had three jail cells that were most often used to house the mentally ill. A hospital wing was added in 1892, funded partly by a $4,000 provincial grant. Source: "If these walls could speak," Wellington County Museum and Archives, Wellington.ca

135 "If these walls could speak." Wellington County Museum and Archives. Wellington.ca

136 Ibid.

137 Oliver Wainwright, "Poor Doors not the worst thing about social housing." *The Guardian*. 30 July 2014. Poor doors have also been suggested for social housing units in Canada, but the roots are in segregation. Appropriate? If not in London, they can they be acceptable in the Promised Land created to eliminate them? Accessed: http://www.theguardian.com/artanddesign/architecture-design-blog/2014/jul/30/poor-door-social-housing-apartheid

138 Workhouse.org http://www.workhouses.org.uk/intro/

139 "Brutal Treatment of the Unemployed, A letter to the editor," *Toronto Star*.

140 Phyllis Harrison, ed. *The Home Children: Their Personal Stories*. Winnipeg: J.Gordon Shillingford Publishing, 1979. p. 7.

141 Ibid.

142 Ibid. p. 75.

143 Ibid. There were so many problems that eventually the Children's Homes forced farmers to send the children's wages to the Home, to be held in trust for the children. One man reported that his 'fortune' for six years of labour was $70.
144 Ibid. p. 19.
145 Ibid. p. 74.
146 Palmer and Heroux, "Cracking the Stone" The authors describe a series of financial collapses beginning from the 1830s to 1929. Their Marxist framework does not quite fit the Canadian economy. During this period, most workers were farmers, shopkeepers and small-town tradesmen.
147 Back to the Land was a movement that believed the unemployed could find better futures by homesteading on the bush and prairie frontier.
148 Palmer and Gaétan Heroux. "Cracking the Stone"
149 Rural Ontarians, in particular, those of Scots descent had been moving to the territories that now comprise northern Ontario, Manitoba, Saskatchewan, and Alberta since the 1870s.
150 Palmer and Heroux, "Cracking the Stone."
151 Ibid.
152 Ibid. The House of Industry had a ward "where men could be put up for the night in a casual ward, get a hot bath, hair doused in vermin-killing liquid solution, and their clothes fumigated, "cleansed and classified" in the vernacular of poor relief officialdom." Prior to the fumigation process being implemented, Toronto's House of Industry had drawn complaints of "sickening smell."
153 Ibid.
154 Prior to 1791, Upper and Lower Canada were united as the Province of Quebec.
155 Palmer and Heroux, "Cracking the Stone."
156 Ibid.
157 Ibid.
158 Ibid.
159 Ibid.
160 Barbara Murphy. *On the Street: How We Created the Homeless.* J. Gordon Shillingford Publishing, Winnipeg, 2000. p. 23. Murphy confirms that Canada remained a rural country longer than the United States or Europe. In the mid 19th century, Montreal had a population of 57,000 (254,000 at the end of the century) and Toronto had a population of only 30,000 (180,000 at end of the century). In 1911, Winnipeg had only 135,000 inhabitants while Vancouver had just over 100,000.

161 Between 1853 and 1857, the City of Guelph's population grew from 2,000 to 4,500. On January 1, 1856, the Council was granted town status. The Council then became responsible for policing, street lighting and maintenance, regulation of alms and workhouses, regulation and licensing of stables and public conveyances, assessment of real estate taxes for local improvements, imposition of fines and limited jail terms for by-law infractions. Source: City of Guelph fonds, accessed: http://www.archeion.ca/city-of-guelph-fonds;rad

162 Canada's motto, *A Mari Usque ad Mare* (from sea to sea) is from Psalms 72:8, and the Biblical scripture, 'they desired a better country' (found on Order of Canada medals) is also carved on Canada's Parliament. (Hebrews 11:16)

163 "Am I my brother's keeper?" comes from Genesis 4:9. The colonists would have known this scripture and the imperative to take care of others.

164 Tyler, Tracey, Legal Affairs Reporter, "When 'poorhouse' wasn't only an expression," *Toronto Star*, 03 January 2009. Accessed: http://www.thestar.com/news/2009/01/03/when_poorhouse_wasnt_only_an_expression.html

165 Housing or jailing the poor to keep them off the streets was called indoor relief.

166 Boucher, Margaret Ruttan (Scott) Biography.ca http://www.biographi.ca/en/bio/boucher_margaret_ruttan_16E.html

167 "Margaret Scott," St. John's Cathedral. Scott is buried at St. John's Cathedral in Winnipeg. Her bio appears on the church website. Accessed: http://stjohnscathedral.ca/about/our-past/cemetery/margaret-scott/

168 Murphy, *The Ugly Canadian, The Rise and Fall of a Caring Society*, J. Gordon Shillingford Publishing, Inc., 1999.

169 While it has moved away from its populist roots, I include the New Democratic Party under this category. The roots of the NDP's predecessor can be found in the Prairie-based populist Commonwealth Cooperative Federation Party as well in the Labour Movement. This social democratic party grew up alongside other Prairie populist parties, including the Social Credit Party and United Farmers of Alberta. While we think of Prairie-based populist parties as right wing, they usually have some form of income redistribution at their heart. This includes modern populist parties such as the Wildrose Party in Alberta and the Saskatchewan Party. While conservative in some respects, these parties have at their heart populist issues such as rural health care, property rights, and education. Those interested in modern populist platforms might start by looking at the platform of modern populist parties, such as the Wildrose Party and the Saskatchewan Party.

170 Murphy, *On the Street* and *The Ugly Canadian*.

171 Researcher David Macdonald used Statistics Canada data to arrive at this figure.

172 Picture ID costs vary widely across Canada. It costs $44 in New Brunswick, $35 in Ontario, $51.45 in Alberta, and $17.20 in Nova Scotia.
173 Emilie Kitteringham, "Where is Albertans' compassion for less fortunate?" Letter to the editor, *Lethbridge Herald,* July 13, 2014.
174 Alberta Human Services, Government of Alberta figures for Income Support. Single, Adult, Able to work. Accessed at: http://humanservices.alberta.ca/financial-support/3171.html
175 "When the Middle Class Becomes Homeless." Video. Accessed: https://www.youtube.com/watch?v=Dk_iiVgJi6A
176 Murphy, *On the Street*, p. 82. Aboriginals who migrate to urban areas face the same problem of all migrants—lack of support.
177 Ibid. p. 82.
178 Ibid. p. 76.
179 Ibid. p. 21.
180 Pete Evans. "Less than Half of Canadians with Disabilities Have Jobs—Statscan," CBC News, Dec 03, 2014 Accessed: http://www.cbc.ca/news/business/less-than-half-of-canadian-adults-with-disabilities-have-jobs-statscan-1.2858954
181 Aly Thomson. "Extremely low number of people with disabilities in politics, professor says Saturday," Canadian Press, July 19th 2014. Accessed: http://www.thecanadianpress.com/english/online/OnlineFullStory.aspx?filename=DOR-MNNCP.2728ee57e0284876aa4b21fd0bbb21a4.CPKEY2008111303&newsitemid=29191009&languageid=1
182 Murphy, *On the Street*, p. 14.
183 Ibid. p. 79.
184 Ibid. p. 84. A 1999 Edmonton task force found that of 800 homeless individuals 42% were aboriginal.
185 Ibid. p. 13. Murphy states that at the turn of 21st century, 29 percent of the homeless in Toronto were women.
186 Ibid. p. 79.
187 If a parent is too poor to afford an apartment, children may not be able to spend weekends with that parent. Many single adults on income support will not be able to find accommodation that will allow their children to spend weekends with them. Most public housing authorities do not allow parents who do not have their children with them full-time the right to live in public housing meant for families. In addition, many municipalities discriminate against parents who do not have full custody of their children by refusing them family discounts and family passes for recreation facilities and public libraries.

188 Jeanette Waegemakers Shiff, PhD. and Alina Turner, PhD., "Alberta Rural Homelessness Report," Turner Research and Strategy, Inc., Alberta Centre for Child, Family, and Community Research & University of Calgary, faculty of social work. June 2014

189 "Poverty Profile Snapshot," Government of Canada. Accessed: http://www.esdc.gc.ca/eng/communities/reports

190 *Fergus News Record,* 20 April 1882, p. 2

191 When I discovered that Robert Boyle had been dragged to death, I shared the information with my mother and her siblings. They already knew the story, and they were quick to tell me that it was their grandfather's fault because he had frightened the horse. They also insisted that the incident had had no effect on their grandfather, although his failures and lost inheritances are now family legends.

192 Mary Ann Smith, my great-grandmother, was the daughter of Richard Smith and Ellen Falls. Richard Smith was the brother of Michael Smith, Barbara Gilchrist's first husband. Therefore, Thomas Smith and Mary Ann Warner Smith, originally from Leicestershire, England, UK are also my great-great-great grandparents. Ellen Falls was the daughter of William Falls, an Enniskillin Dragoon wounded at Waterloo, and Ellen Wray, of Enniskillin, Northern Ireland, UK. The Falls came to Canada when William Falls received a medal and a land grant in Canada for his efforts at Waterloo.

193 Norman is recorded as working for his Uncle Adam in Garafaxa in 1911, the year his grandmother Barbara died. He is listed as a servant, not a family member. By then my great-grandfather had lost his inheritance. Norman is 15 years old, but he is not in school. One can only speculate on the family politics and the environment that prompted my grandfather to leave Ontario as a teenager to take a homestead as his grandfather William Boyle had done when he left Ulster in the 1840s. The family had by World War I divided into 'haves' and 'have nots.'

194 The 1916 Census records 20-year-old Norman farming on his own in Alberta. He's calling himself a Presbyterian and giving his ethnicity as English. His mother was English and his Gilchrist relatives were Presbyterian. Perhaps, Norman is distancing himself from his father's family. Accessed: http://data2.collectionscanada.ca/006003/t-21947/jpg/31228_4363976-00530.jpg

195 Homestead Record, Section 34, Township 48, Range 10, Film #2400 in Accession #1970.313, Provincial Archives of Alberta. While he didn't sign up for WW I, like his brother William, he did catch the influenza the soldiers brought home in 1919. He survived. Many in Alberta did not.

196 "The Adverse Childhood Experiences Study." Accessed: http://www.acestudy.org.

197 Elizabeth K. Hopper, Ellen L. Bassuk, and Jeffrey Olivet, "Shelter from the Storm: Trauma-Informed Care in Homelessness Services Settings," *The Open Health Services and Policy Journal*, 2009, pp. 131–151.
198 Ibid.
199 Ibid.
200 Christians Against Poverty. This non-profit ministry assists people out of personal debt in the UK, Australia and New Zealand. CAP opened their Canadian office in March 2013 in response to requests from Canadian churches who saw a need for debt counselling in their cities. https://www.capcanada.org
201 Tough love is a phrase that means using harsh treatment to 'help someone.' In cases of addiction, it may help stop the downward spiral, but only if it is combined with true concern for the individual. However, tough love has also been linked to authoritarian parenting, child abuse, and abuse by authority figures, such as school coaches. I discovered a tough love approach, for example: intrusive questions, making trauma victims repeat their story over and over again in order to determine whether they are one of the 'deserving poor,' an almost universal approach when I tried to get help after I was injured in 2013. Medical professionals, Human Services Workers, and the local food bank wanted me to relive the crisis over and over again, so they could determine if I really needed help. I even had to show picture ID and explain my circumstance in detail to get food. In the end, I decided that dealing with helping agencies was doing me more harm than good. In my experience, a tough love approach after trauma is not only shaming, it triggers panic, more shame, and even thoughts of suicide.
202 Real estate matters are dealt with in lower-level Master-In-Chambers sessions and the judge is called a Master. The Court of Queen's Bench is also the Superior Trial Court in Alberta.
203 Brad Tuttle, "Foreclosures, House Flipping is Hot Again,"*Time*, 16 October, 2012.
204 The real estate business markets to flippers, not only in large cities, but in the suburbs and smaller communities through websites such as Lethbridge House Flippers and http://www.viewlethbridge.com/lethbridgeforeclosures.html
205 Murphy, *On the Street*, p. 20.
206 Michael Babad, "How speculators fed U.S. housing bubble, fuelled bust, *The Globe and Mail*, 16 Dec. 16 2011, and Shelley Youngblut, "What will make the housing boom go bust? 'Greed'," *The Globe and Mail*, 14 April 2012.
207 Roma Luciw, "Canadians spend more income on housing than almost anyone in the world," *The Globe and Mail*, Thursday, 30 October 2014.

208 "Black Rock Survey: Canadians Prioritize Long-Term Financial Goals, but Their Short-Term Actions Are a Barrier to Reaching Them" http://www.marketwired.com/press-release/blackrock-survey-canadians-prioritize-long-term-financial-goals-but-their-short-term-1962637.htm

209 Roma Luciw, "Canadians spend more income on housing than almost anyone in the world," *The Globe and Mail*, Thursday, 30 October 2014.

210 Squatting has become an increasingly popular act of defiance against inadequate housing. Some activist organizations prepare information guides for squatters. But squatting is nothing new. In colonial British North America and late 19th-Century Canada, the poor often squatted in shacks along river banks and in rural areas with little disruption. The Peterborough Coalition Against Poverty Guide for Squatters, published by the Centre Social Autogere in 2003, online: http://www.centresocialautogere.org/sites/default/files/upload/PCAPsquattersGuideFINALJune2003.pdf

211 Michael Franklin, "City of Calgary to Close Midfield Mobile Home Park," CTV Calgary 27 May 2014.

212 "Social Agencies Worry over fate of Midfield residents," *Calgary Herald*.

213 Oscar Douglas Skelton, *The Life and Times of Sir Alexander Tilloch Galt*, Oxford University Press: Toronto, 1920.

214 "Medicine Hat Renter Woes." Video Clip. CTV News, Calgary. May 2015. Accessed: http://calgary.ctvnews.ca/video?clipId=394240&binId=1.1484062&playlistP.Num=1

215 Murphy, *On the Street*. p. 13.

216 Ibid. p. 98.

217 Ibid. pp. 37–38.

218 Ibid. p. 30.

219 Ibid. pp. 30–31.

220 According to the content on "EV Experience, River Walk," on Calgary East Village's website: evexperience.com, "River Walk promises homebuyers "dedicated pedestrian and cycle lanes wind their way along the edge of the Bow and Elbow rivers, dotted by restful benches nestled among naturalized vegetation."

221 "Bringing Lethbridge Home, 2013 Homeless Census Report," prepared for Social Housing in Action by: The Community and Social Development Group, City of Lethbridge with assistance from: Jerry Firth, Practicum Student, Faculty of Social Work University of Calgary Southern Alberta Region, November 2013, Accessed at http://www.bringinglethbridgehome.ca/sites/default/files/Bringing%20Lethbridge%20Home%20-%20Homeless%20Census%20Report%202013.pdf

222 City of Lethbridge Census, City of Lethbridge, 2013. Lethbridge had 90,417 people in 2013, according to the City of Lethbridge Census, released in July 2013.
223 Leslie Ferenc, "Canada Failing Homeless Youth, Report Charges, *Toronto Star*, 3 March 3, 2014. Accessed: http://yfile.news.yorku.ca/2014/03/03/canadas-under-35s-are-also-rans-in-the-wealth-race/
224 Murphy, *On the Street*. p. 87.
225 Nan Roman and Lisa Stand, *The Homeless Hub*, Spring 2012.
226 "Medicine Hat Plan to End Homelessness, January Update," *The Homeless Hub*, January 2014.
227 A year after my injury, I finally got a hearing test. Apparently, I could have had one several months before, but no one told me that the service was available until August 2014.
228 Clients are given three-month membership cards and must prove they are still in need to get them renewed. By October I had enough funding to finish my book, as well as fall workshops to teach, so I was happy not to have to renew my membership.
229 "All Foods Fit: Food Banks Canada Statement on the Types of Food Distributed by Food Banks." News Release, Food Banks Canada. 21 August 2014. Food Banks Canada says the goal is to provide the same food you see in grocery carts—items like pasta and sauce, fresh fruit and vegetables, breakfast cereals, and even cookies and cake. Given that food banks rely on donations, this is a challenge.
230 Fifty percent of people who need food banks but stay away out of shame. Source: Community Food Centres.
231 "Hunger Count 2014," Food Banks Canada, Accessed: http://www.foodbankscanada.ca/getmedia/7739cdff-72d5-4cee-85e9-54d456669564/HungerCount_2014_EN.pdf.aspx?ext=.pdf
232 Michael Ferguson, "2014 Fall Report of the Auditor General of Canada, Auditor General's Opening Statement," 2014 Fall Report Press Conference, Auditor General of Canada.
233 Hunger Count 2014, Food Banks Canada.
234 Ken Dryden, Special to the *Star*, "Edited interview with Nick Saul, president of Community Food Centres Canada, former head of The Stop," *Toronto Star*, 30 June 2014.
235 The Stop Website: http://www.thestop.org/
236 Community Food Centres Canada Website: http://cfccanada.ca/
237 Nick Saul, "Community Food Centres Canada, Good Food is just the beginning." Newsletter, 29 December 2014, p. 1.
238 Ibid.

239 "Community Gardens," The Stop Website. Accessed http://thestop.org/node/68/community-gardens

240 "Make Something Edmonton.ca details plans for Edmontons's 1ˢᵗ River Valley Food Forest:" Make Something Edmonton. Accessed: http://www.makesomethingedmonton.ca/projects/506-edmontons-1st-river-valley-food-forest/

241 "Inspiring Education Through Agriculture," Sustainable Food Edmonton. Accessed: http://sustainablefoodedmonton.org/urban-ag-high/inspiring-education-through-urban-agriculture/

242 Debora Van Brenk, "Food Folly, What a waste," *The London Free Press*, 9 July 19, 2014. http://www.lfpress.com/2014/07/09/what-a-waste

243 Philippa Willets, "March of the Food Snobs," *Disability Intersections*, 22 January 2014. Accessed: http://disabilityintersections.com/2014/01/march-of-the-food-snobs/

244 According to Potatogoodness.com, a potato has only 110 calories, and is high in fibre, Vitamin C, potassium, and Vitamin B6. Accessed: http://www.potatogoodness.com/nutrition/nutritional-facts/

245 "Global Demand for Quinoa Takes Toll on Andean Farmers and Consumers," *Global Voices Online*, 6 November 2013. Accessed: http://globalvoicesonline.org/2013/11/06/global-demand-for-quinoa-takes-toll-on-andean-farmers-and-consumers/

246 Several months later, in January, fearing eviction from my home, I was well enough to meet with an outreach worker at the YWCA to figure out next steps. She seemed to feel that, because I was actually not homeless yet, that I was in pretty good shape. She even asked me what ideas I had for my future. I don't think told her I was thinking of jumping off the bridge. To be fair, the YWCA Executive Director, who knew me from my days on the Board of directors of that organization, did offer her support when Alberta Human Services could not find my Health Benefit application.

247 "Alison Redford's Controversial Sky Palace Actually Cost Taxpayers More than $93,000 Wildrose says," *National Post*, 10 September 2014.

248 "Alberta Communication Staff Cost of $23 Million," *The Huffington Post Alberta*, 4 April 2014. Accessed: http://www.huffingtonpost.ca/2014/04/04/alberta-communications-staff_n_5091565.html and Jen Gerson, "Alberta's $21 M media strategy employs scores more staff than actual reporters covering government," *National Post*, 3 April, 2014. Accessed: http://news.nationalpost.com/2014/04/03/alberta-spends-21m-per-year-on-communications-staff-employs-many-more-people-than-reporters-covering-government/

249 The Mandate of Alberta Human Services is a standard one for the poverty industry—lots of talk about 'partners' and 'core business' and

'stakeholders'—but well thought out 'mandates' don't mean a whole lot to the people trying to just keep their life on track. In fact, disconnect between the 'bureaucratic' nature of government and the immediate needs of people to solve their problems collide. Most people don't want to wait another month to come back for another meeting about the same issue. What place does clichéd business jargon like 'work collaboratively' and 'core business' offering services to vulnerable populations? Accessed: http://humanservices.alberta.ca/department.html

250 Human Services, Government of Alberta. Accessed: http://humanservices.alberta.ca/financial-support/3171.html

251 The Organization Chart for Alberta Human Services is not usually complicated when it comes to bureaucracy, but it's hard to see where the clients come in or how a complicated bureaucracy can assist people at the worst time in their lives when simplicity and low stress are paramount to getting back on track. Accessed: http://humanservices.alberta.ca/documents/Organizational-Chart.pdf

252 I am not sure what happened on this occasion, but I was almost struck by a car crossing the street several times in the first year after my injury. This was probably one of those times, but it's also possible that this is one of the times I slipped on the ice. Fatigue and dizziness have been an issue since I was hurt.

253 "Contribution to Reducing Poverty in Canada Brief to the House of Commons Standing Committee on Human Resources, Skills and Social Development and the Status of Persons with Disabilities (HUMA)," Canadian Nurses Association, Ottawa, Ontario June 10, 2009, Canadian Nurses Association Accessed: http://cna-aiic.ca/~/media/cna/page-content/pdf-fr/reducing_poverty_e.pdf Federal

254 "National pharmacare plan could save up to $10.7 billion a year: study," News Release, Canadian Centre for Policy Alternatives, 13 September 2010. Accessed: http://www.policyalternatives.ca/newsroom/news-releases/national-pharmacare-plan-could-save-107-billion-year-study.

255 Ibid.

256 The Prentice government did bring in a Premium Plan in the Spring 2015 budget, but the plan was different from the previous one. Incomes under $50,000 are exempt and the plan will be administered through the income tax deductions if it ever becomes law.

257 "Alberta to end health care premiums, Alberta's Conservative government will eliminate health care premiums entirely on Jan. 1, Finance Minister Iris Evans announced today in her provincial budget," *Edmonton Journal*, 22 April 2008.

258 Chandra Lye. "Alberta Health Minister surprised after PC Party delegates vote in favour of health care premiums," CTV Edmonton 24 November 2013.

259 Mariam Ibrahim, "Boost Alberta Legal Aid or face 'potentially devastating' consequences, CEO says," *Edmonton Journal*, 17 June 2014. Accessed: http://www.edmontonjournal.com/touch/story.html?id=9944389

260 Jason Van Rassell, "Banff Meeting Offers Minister Opportunity to Press Ottawa for Legal Aid Funding," *Calgary Herald*. Accessed: http://www.calgaryherald.com/news/Banff+meeting+offers+ministers+opportunity+press+Ottawa+legal+funding/10292916/story.html. (Link no longer available.)

261 Since 2011, Alberta has had five premiers: Ed Stelmach (December 14, 2006-October 7, 2011), Alison Redford (October 7, 2011-March 23, 2014), Dave Hancock (March 23, 2014-September 15, 2014), Jim Prentice (September 15, 2014 to 24, 2015) and the current premier, Rachel Notley who took office May 24, 2015.

262 "Legal Aid Funding to Increase in Alberta. Province Commits More Money and will increase upper limit for eligibility," CBC News, 30 October 2014. Accessed: http://www.cbc.ca/news/canada/calgary/legal-aid-funding-to-increase-in-alberta-1.2818806

263 Murphy, *On the Street*, p. 20.

264 Alan Pyke, "Impoverished Mother Dies in Jail Cell Over Unpaid Fines For Her Kids Missing School," *Think Progress*. 12 June 2014. Accessed: http://thinkprogress.org/economy/2014/06/12/3448105/mother-dies-jail-cell-fines/

265 Joseph Shapiro, "Increasing Court Fees Punish the Poor," *National Public Radio*. 19 May 2014. Accessed: http://www.npr.org/2014/05/19/312158516/increasing-court-fees-punish-the-poor

266 Bank Rate.co lists the "Top Ten Causes of Debt." Several of them are not related to planning, work ethic, or financial literacy. http://www.bankrate.com/finance/debt/top-10-causes-of-debt-1.aspx#ixzz3Leg4CARM

267 Kathy Tomlinson. *Go Public*, "Scotiabank hit injured soldier with $7K mortgage penalty, Bank apologizes, cancels fee after Go Public takes on story," CBC News posted: 24 June 2014. http://www.cbc.ca/news/canada/ottawa/scotiabank-hit-injured-soldier-with-7k-mortgage-penalty-1.2684694

268 Keith Leslie reported on this story for CTV News, explaining how Money Mart attracted outrage for a plan to take 50% of the value of gift cards in exchange for cash. http://www.ctvnews.ca/politics/ont-ndp-pc-blast-money-mart-s-50-cash-for-gift-card-fee-1.2133206#ixzz3LekxuaU6

269 "Lethbridge City Council has agreed to ask the Province to change the regulations governing 'Quick Cash' stores," CJOC-FM. October http://www.cjocfm.com/news-and-info/news/lethbridge-news/lethbridge-city-council-discusses-concerns-around-payday-loans-stores/

270 Jacqueline Nelson, "Insurers Demand Government Change One Year After Alberta's Floods," *The Globe and Mail*, 20 June 2014.

271 Kristian Bonn, "Insurance Company Profits for 2012 $4.4 Billion," *Bonn Law Blawg*, Bonnlaw.ca, 21 March 2013. Accessed: http://bonnlaw.ca/2013/03/21/insurance-company-profits-for-2012-4-4-billion/

272 Peter Cheney, "Why Ontario Drivers Pay the Highest Car Insurance Rates in the Country," *The Globe and Mail*, 9 July 2014.

273 Caroline Zenter, "Minimum Wage is not Enough, Lethbridge has the second highest number of low-wage workers among Alberta cities," *Lethbridge Herald*, 31 August 2013, p. 1.

274 Janelle-Vandergrift, "Why Poor People Just Can't Get a Job,"*Huffington Post Canada*, 25 June 2014. Accessed: http://www.huffingtonpost.ca/janelle-vandergrift/poverty-jobs_b_5529331.html

275 "Poverty Trend Highlights; Canada 2013," Canadians For Public Justice, October 2014. Accessed: http://cpj.ca/sites/default/files/docs/Poverty-Trends-Highlights-2013.pdf

276 Michelle Fleury, "Obama's plans to make US companies pay staff overtime," BBC News, 13 March 2014. Accessed: http://www.bbc.com/news/business-26560262.

277 "Underemployment is Canada's Real Labour Market Challenge," Canadian Labour Congress. Thursday, 6 March 2014. Accessed: http://www.canadianlabour.ca/news-room/publications/underemployment-canadas-real-labour-market-challenge

278 "A Survey of Employment Standard Violations," Workers Action Centre, Toronto, ON May 2011, Accessed: http://www.workersactioncentre.org/wpcontent/uploads/2011/12/pb_unpaidwagesunprotectedworkers_eng.pdf

279 BMO Chief Economist, BMO Capital Markets; "Skills Shortages? We've Seen Worse…Much Worse," BMO Nesbitt Burns, April 2, 2013. Accessed: http://www.bmonesbittburns.com/economics/amcharts/apro213.pdf

280 J.C Herbert Emery, Department of Economics, University of Calgary; "Labour Shortages in Saskatchewan," SPP Research Papers, School of Public Policy, University of Calgary, Volume 6, Issue 4, January 2013.

281 Emery, "Labour Shortages in Saskatchewan."

282 Laura Payton, "Temporary Foreign Worker Program faces renewed call for audit, Confusion over labour data comes as Liberals repeat call for auditor general probe," CBC News, 05 May 2014. Accessed: http://www.cbc.ca/news/politics/temporary-foreign-worker-program-faces-renewed-call-for-audit-1.2632231

283 Geoff Leo, "Advice to Saskatchewan firm 'intimidating' to foreign workers, law prof says email about 'Canadianized' employees not a threat, owner insists" CBC News, 5 May 2014.

284 BMO Chief Economist, BMO Capital Markets; "Skills Shortages? We've Seen Worse...Much Worse," BMO Nesbitt Burns, April 2, 2013. Accessed: http://www.bmonesbittburns.com/economics/amcharts/apro213.pdf

285 Randall Bartlett and Helen Lao on behalf of Canada's Parliamentary Budget Officer, "Labour Market Assessment 2014," 25 March 25 2014 Accessed: http://www.pbo-dpb.gc.ca/files/files/Labour_Note_EN.pdf

286 Derek Burleton, Sonya Gulati, Connor McDonald, and Sonny Scarfone, "Jobs in Canada, Where, What and For Whom," TD Bank, October 22, 2013.

287 "New study on labour market shows that there is no widespread labour shortage," News Release, Alberta Federation of Labour, Friday 04 July 2014. Accessed: http://www.afl.org/index.php/Press-Release/low-wage-employers-in-alberta-are-blowing-smoke-when-they-whine-about-labour-shortages.html

288 Dominique M. Gross, Professor, School of Public Policy, Simon Fraser University prepared this report on labour shortages for the C.D. Howe Institute, Commentary 407. "Temporary Foreign Workers in Canada: Are they really filling labour shortages?" April 2014.

289 "Alberta relying on bogus labour-shortage figures," News Release, Alberta Federation of Labour, 25 July 2012. Accessed: http://www.afl.org/index.php/Press-Release/alberta-relying-of-bogus-labour-shortage-figures.html

290 Susan McDaniel, Bonnie Watt-Malcolm, and Lloyd Wong, "Is the Math Sufficient? Aging Workforce and the Future Labour Market in Canada," Prentice Institute, University of Lethbridge, 15 December 2013. Accessed: http://www.uleth.ca/prenticeinstitute/sites/prenticeinstitute/files/KnowledgeSynthesis%20full%20report%20--McDaniel%20Watt-Malcolm%20Wong.pdf

291 "Canadian Job Market Increasingly a Tale of have and have not occupations: CIBC," CNW, 3 December 2012. Accessed: http://www.newswire.ca/en/story/1082363/canadian-job-market-increasingly-a-tale-of-have-and-have-not-occupations-cibc

292 Susana Mas, "Temporary Foreign Worker Program sanctions Nova Scotia trucking company, Paul Easson doesn't think his company has broken the rules," CBC News, 8 May 2014. Accessed: http://www.cbc.ca/news/politics/temporary-foreign-worker-program-sanctions-nova-scotia-trucking-company-1.2636711

293 "Employers who have broken the rules or been suspended from the Temporary Foreign Worker Program," Employment and Social Development Canada. Accessed: http://www.esdc.gc.ca/eng/jobs/foreign_workers/employers_revoked.shtml

294 Susana Mas, "Temporary foreign worker overhaul imposes limits, hikes inspections, Cap on low-wage temporary workers to be phased in over

two years," CBC News, 20 Jun 20, 2014. Accessed: http://www.cbc.ca/news/politics/temporary-foreign-worker-overhaul-imposes-limits-hikes-inspections-1.2682209

295 Ibid.

296 "Minister for Employment and Social Development Jason Kenney and Minister of Citizenship and Immigration Chris Alexander Hold a News Conference to Make an Announcement on Reforms to the Temporary Foreign Worker Program." Transcription News Conference, Political and Social Affairs Division, Parliament of Canada, Ottawa.

297 Robert Burns, "Auld Lang Syne", 1788. Link: http://www.robertburns.org/works/236.shtml

298 S Gaetz, T Gulliver, T Richter, "The State of Homelessness in Canada," Homeless Hub, Accessed at http://www.homelesshub.ca/SOHC2014

299 Stephanie Levitz, "$46 per Canadian a year could drastically reduce homelessness: report, October 29, 2014." The Canadian Press. Accessed at CTV News: http://www.ctvnews.ca/canada/46-per-canadian-a-year-could-drastically-reduce-homelessness-report-1.2076556.

300 Harvey Stevens, "A Proposal for Reforming Social Security for Non-Elderly Adults in Canada." Basic Income Canada, Winnipeg, March 2014.

301 Evelyn L. Forget, "The Town With No Poverty, Using Health Administration Data to Revisit Outcomes of a Canadian Guaranteed Annual Income Field Experiment." The University of Manitoba, February 2011. Accessed: http://public.econ.duke.edu/~erw/197/forget-cea%20(2).pdf

302 Tim Rourke. "The Manitoba Mincome Study; Even a small Guaranteed Income has dramatic positive effects on society Citizen's Income," Toronto - Oct. 2009 http://www.livableincome.org/atrmincome.htm

303 Michael Ferguson, Auditor General of Canada, 2014 Fall Report of the Auditor General of Canada, Auditor General's Opening Statement, 2014 Fall Report Press Conference. Also reported in CBC Inside Politics Blog, "WWI soldiers' files being digitized by Library and Archives Canada Archives begins painstaking process of getting its most-requested items online." Susan Lunn, CBC News Posted: Dec 25, 2014 9:00 PM ET Last Updated: Dec 25, 2014 9:00 PM ET. Ferguson was discussing the bad connect between several federal government agencies reviewed in his Fall 2014 Report, but his comment applies well across Canada's federal and provincial bureaucracies.

304 Michael Ferguson, Auditor General of Canada, 2014 Fall Report of the Auditor General of Canada, Auditor General's Opening Statement, 2014 Fall Report Press Conference.

305 Community Food Centres Canada, "Mapping the Possibilities of Food," Community Food Centres Canada, 2013–14 Progress Report, December 2014, Accessed: http://cfccanada.ca/sites/default/files/documents/CFCC_2013-14ProgressReport_FINAL_web.pdf

306 Canada's motto, 'A Mari Usque ad Mare (from sea to sea)' is from Psalms 72:8. The Biblical scripture, 'they desired a better country' (Hebrews 11:16) is inscribed on Order of Canada medals and carved on Canada's Parliament.

307 Barbara's daughter-in-law, Mary Ann Smith Boyle was the granddaughter of William Falls, a Napoleonic War veteran who received a land grant in the colony. His son, James Falls, appears to have moved to Garafraxa sometime in the 1840's seeking his own land. His much younger daughter, Ellen (my great-great-grandmother), may have lived with her brother's family prior to her marriage to Richard Smith.

308 "Reading,"*East Garafraxa, A History, The Corporation of the Township of East Garafraxa*, Steven J. Brown and A. Krista Taylor, 2006.

309 Matthew Shaw, *Great Scots! : How the Scots Created Canada*, Heartland Associates, Winnipeg, 2003, p. 10.

310 Murphy, *On the Street*, p. 126.

311 *The Gifts of Imperfection, Let Go of Who You Think You're Supposed to Be and Embrace Who You Are*, Brené Brown, Ph.D. L.M.S.W. (Hazelden, 2010), p. 20.

312 Greg Weadick was the Member of the Legislative Assembly for Lethbridge West until Shannon Philips defeated him in the May 5, 2015, NDP sweep of Lethbridge's provincial ridings. Weadick's office was a three-minute walk from the Canada Alberta Service Centre in Lethbridge. Greg Weadick supported Mr. Jim Prentice's bid to lead the Alberta Progressive Conservatives, but once he became premier, Mr. Prentice removed Mr. Weadick from cabinet, a move that may have contributed to the magnitude of the defeat of PC candidates in Lethbridge and rural ridings surrounding the city received May 5, 2015.

313 My maternal grandmother was the widow of Barbara Gilchrist's grandson, Norman Boyle. While she married into the dominant culture she remained proudly Swedish. She was raised near Jarvie, Alberta. However, many Swedes also homesteaded near the Ontario-born homesteaders in Minburn County, East Central Alberta.

314 From my notes, written on the anniversary of the night before the 2013 flood.

INDEX

Abbotsford, 31
Aboriginal peoples
   living in poverty, 29, 79
   Marlene Bird, 30
   as social exile, 15–16, 34
Adult Heath Benefit Card, 106
Adverse Childhood Experiences Study, 82
Agricultural workers, 61–64
Alberta
   flood day, 37, 39, 110
   Legal Aid, 106–107
   Redford government, 100
Alberta Adult Health Benefit, 103
Alberta Federation of Labour, 116, 117
Alberta Health Benefit, 104
Alberta Health Services (AHS), 105
Alberta Human Services, 101, 102
Alberta Income for the Severely Handicapped (AISH), 101, 107
Alberta Rural Homelessness Report (Waegemakers Schiff & Turner), 79
Alberta Works, 101, 102, 103, 104, 131, 132, 135
Allen, Jimmy, 59
"Am I remembered in Erin?" (McGee), 19–20
Annual Homeless Count 2013 (SHIA), 92

Apprenticeship training, 114–115
Attainable Homes Calgary Corporation, 87
Auditor General's Report, Fall 2014, 96–97, 122–123
Auld lang syne (Burns), 119–120
Auto insurance, 110
Avenue Living, 88–89

Bank of Canada Business Outlook Survey, 116
Banks, chartered, 109–110
Basic Income Canada Network, 122
Battle of Waterloo, 23
Benefits, 112–113
Bird, Marlene, 30
Black Rock Asset Management, 85
Blight, potato, 14
BMC Medicine, 27
Bond Head, Francis, 66
Boyle, Adam, 51, 52
Boyle, Alfred, 51, 52, 57
Boyle, Barbara. *See* Gilchrist, Barbara
Boyle, Charles, 50, 52
Boyle, Maria Kennedy, 50–53
Boyle, Mary Jane, 50, 52
Boyle, Norman, 81
Boyle, Robert, 51, 80
Boyle, Samuel, 51, 52, 80–81

Boyle, Sophia, 51, 52, 53
Boyle, Thomas, 50, 52
Boyle, William James, 50–53, 56, 57, 64
Brain Injury Rehabilitation Services, 93
Britain
   home children, 61–64, 115
   Poor Law Amendment Act, 25
   Scottish settlers and, 22–24, 26
British Broadcasting Corporation (BBC), 111
British House of Industry, 60
Brown, Brené, 126–127
Burns, Robert, 119–120

Calgary, 30–31, 86
Campey, Lucille H., 23
Canada, housing costs in, 85
Canada/Alberta Service Centre, 44
Canada Company, 87–88, 126
Canadian Alliance to End Homelessness, 121
Canadian Centre for Policy Alternatives, 75, 104
Canadian Department of Agriculture, home children and, 61
Canadian Imperial Bank of Commerce (CIBC), 117
Canadian Institute of Health Research, 103–104
Canadian Labour Congress, 111–112
Canadian Public Health Insurance, 74
Car insurance, 110
Cash store, 110
C.D. Howe Institute, 116
Cell, 27
Certified General Accountants of Canada, 117
Charity, 11
Cheshire, Tom, 26
Children
   home, 61–64, 115

poorhouse, 57, 59–60, 70
poverty, 76
See also Youth
Christians Against Poverty, 83
Citizens for Public Justice, 29, 79
Coderre, Denis, 31
Collection agencies, 108–109
Community
   assistance from, 34, 53
   creating, 59, 92–93, 97–99, 126–127
   gardens, 98
   Scottish, 28–29
   social exiles as members of, 107–108
Community Food Centres Canada (CFCC), 97–98
Conference Board of Canada, 32
Connor, Bridget, 24
Conservatism, Canadian, 74
Consumers Association of Canada (CAC), 110
Creature Sightings, 30

Dalhousie settlement, 88
Dauphin, Manitoba, 121–122
David and Goliath, Underdogs, Misfits, and the Art of Battling Giants (Gladwell), 133
Death, isolation and, 28
Debt, 109–110
De-institutionalization, 92
Deserving poor
   attitudes towards, 75–76
   food banks and, 95, 97–98
   in 19th Century Canada, 69–72
   poorhouse, 58
De Vere, Stephen E., 25
Diefenbaker, John George, 74
Disability Supplement, 109
Divorce, 34, 109

Edmonton, 98
Edmonton Journal, 106–107

Emery, Herb, 114–115
Everson, Julia, 59–60
Exchange, 113
Exile, defined, 19
　See also Social exile
The Explorer Gene (Cheshire), 26

Famine, Irish, 25
Farm workers, 61–64
Fergus, 10, 14
Fergus News Record, 52
Ferguson, Michael, 96–97, 122–123
Financial Services industry, 109–110
Food banks, 93–99, 131
Food Banks and the Dependence Myth (Food Banks Canada), 95
Food snobbery, 99
Food waste, 99
Foreclosure, 84, 85, 86
Franklin, John, 20–21
Free Market Ideology, 74

Galt, Alexander, 26, 74
Galt, John, 87
Gambling, 109
Garafraxa district
　death of Robert Boyle, 80
　Gilchrists arrive in, 14
　real estate market, 88, 126
　William Boyle, 50–53
　Woolners in, 24
Gene, explorer, 26
Genetics, stress and, 26–27
Gentrification, 85, 91
The Gifts of Imperfection (Brown), 126–127
Gilchrist, Barbara
　childhood, 13–14
　death, 125
　Michael Smith and, 47–50
　widow's weeds, 9–10
　William Boyle and, 50–53, 56, 57

Gilchrist, John, 14–15, 48
Gilchrist, Mary, 14, 47
Gilchrist, Merin, 14
Gilchrist, Samuel, 14, 48
Gilchrist, Sarah, 13, 24, 47, 48
Gilchrist, William, 14, 48, 51
Gladwell, Malcolm, 133
Go Public, 110
Government of Alberta. *See specific departments*
Guaranteed annual income, 121–122, 123–124
Guelph, 10, 53, 60, 125

Hancock, Dave, 117
Harris, Jane
　Alberta Works, 101, 102, 103, 104, 131, 132, 135
　assault and aftermath, 37–46
　brain injury, 42, 43–46, 90, 93, 100, 103, 130–131, 139
　children, 41, 43–44
　empowerment, 130–140
　first marriage, 18
　food Bank, 93–94, 131
　on government labyrinth, 102–106
　health card, 42, 105
　isolation, 43
　night in coffee shop, 15–18
　on the poverty industry, 127–129
　second marriage, 38–39
　as social exile, 32–35
　working poor, 32–33
　writings, 38, 46, 135
Harrison, Phyllis, 62
Hatfield, Christopher, 20
Health care
　access to mental health services, 78, 92, 122
　National Medicare, 75
　premiums, 105–106
　refugees and, 76

Hehr, Kent, 79
Help, asking for, 18, 127–129
  See also Shame
Highlanders, 14, 22, 28
Highland Famine, 25
Highland Society of Canada, 28
Home children, 61–64, 115
The Home Children (Harrison), 62, 63
Homeless
  access to rights and services, 108
  counting the, 92
  Creature Sightings, 30
  housing, 84–88
  mental illness and, 78, 79
  real estate market and, 84–85
  shelters, 75–76
  as social exiles, 15–16, 17, 76–80
  trauma and, 82–83
Homesickness
  "Am I remembered in Erin?," 19–20
  British home children, 62–63
  Scottish colonists, 18, 21
House flipping, 84
Houses of Refuge Act, 57
Housing, 84–88
Housing First, 93
Houston Pizza, 115
Howson, Leonard, 59
Hugh, 112–113

Identity, Scots maintaining in Canada, 29
Immigrants, housing and, 86
Indoor relief, 57, 71, 72, 75–76
An Inquiry into the Causes and Effects of Emigration from the Highlands and Western Isles of Scotland (Irvine), 23
Insurance, 110
Ireland, 25–26
Irvine, Alexander, 23
Isolation
  death and, 28
  illness and, 32, 33
  poverty and, 29–30

Jail, 108
Johnson, Boris, 31
Justice system, poverty and, 106–109

Kenney, Jason, 118
Kismat, Jennifer, 86–87
Klaszus, Jeremy, 31

Labour shortage in Canada
  contemporary, 116–117
  19th Century, 61–64
Land
  cost, in Calgary, 87
  grants, 24
  purchase/sale of, 14, 22, 26, 48, 68, 87–88, 126
Landlord
  for-profit culture, 89, 90
  low-income Canadians, 87, 89
  Scottish, 21, 25
Lang, Amanda, 113
Langmuir, John, 67
Leeson, Manasseh, 48, 126
Legal Aid, 106–107
Lethbridge Herald, 76
Levesque, Mario, 79
Libraries, 28, 29

Macdonald, John A., 74
MacKenzie, Alexander, 22
Manitoba Public Insurance, 110
Manure, 31
Margaret Scott Mission, 71–72
McAlister, John, 48
McAlister, Sarah. *See* Gilchrist, Sarah
McClelland, Mary Jane Boyle, 52
McDaniel, Susan, 117
McDermaid, John, 21

McGee, Thomas D'Arcy, 19–20
McGill University, 27
McGowan, Gil, 117
McLaughlin, Will, 83
Meanie, Michael, 27
Medication expense, 44, 103–104
Medicine Hat, Housing First, 93
Mentally disabled, 78, 79
Metro News, 31
Metz, Gerlinde, 27, 82
Midfield Mobile Home Park, 86
Miller, Thomas, 23
Mobile Urban Street Team (MUST), 17
Money management, poor, 109
Money Mart, 110
Montreal, anti-homeless spikes, 31
Mullainathan, Sendhil, 28
Murphy, Barbara, 30, 78, 79, 108, 126

Napoleonic Wars, 23
National Housing Act, 91
National Medicare, 74
Nature, 28
Negative income tax, 121–122, 123–124
Neighbourhood Improvement Program (NIP), 91
Nesbitt Burns, 116
Netherlands, 85
Niven, Frederick, 20
Northwest Passage, 21
Notley, Rachel, 100, 107
Nunavut, 96
Nutrition North Program, 96–97, 122–123

Obama, Barack, 111
Old Age pensions, 74
Old Man River, 37
Ontario Charity Aid Act, 67
On the Street, How We Created the Homeless (Murphy), 30, 79, 126

Open Health Service and Policy Journal, 82
Outdoor relief, 71–72

Parliamentary Budget Officer, 116
Paupers palaces, 60
Perthshire, Scotland, 21, 23
Physically disabled, 78–79
Polkosnik, Suzanne, 106–107
Poor, attitude towards, 34
  See also Poverty; Social exile
Poorhouse
  life in, 58–60
  mission, 92–93
  in Ontario, 55–57
  See also Food banks; Shelter
Poor law, 26
Poor Law Amendment Act, 25
Post traumatic stress disorder, 45, 46
Potatoes, 14, 25, 97, 99, 136
Poverty
  in 19th Century Canada, 61, 64–72, 76
  children living in, 76
  deserving poor, 58, 69–72, 75–76
  exile and, 19
  Justice system, 106–109
  medication, 103–104
  pre-Confederation solutions, 57
  risk factors for, 29
  rural, 79
  suicide and, 32
  undeserving poor, 67–69, 91
  working poor, 111–113
  See also Social exile
Prentice, Jim, 107
Prentice Institute, 117
Proceedings of the National Academy of Sciences, 28
A Proposal for Reforming Social Security for Non-Elderly Adults in Canada, 122

Quebecor, 31

Real estate market, 84–88, 126
Redford, Alison, 100
Refugee claimants, 76
Regent Park, Toronto, 91, 98
Residential Rehabilitation Assistance Program (RRAP), 91
Rural communities, hunger in, 96–97

Saskatchewan, 114–115
Saul, Nick, 97–98
Scarcity: Why Having Too Little Means So Much (Mullainathan & Shafir), 28
Scotiabank, 110
Scotland
  Auld Lang Syne, 119–120
  Niven on, 20
  Perthshire, 21
Scott, Margaret, 71–72
Scottish colonists
  community in Canada, 28–29
  as social exiles, 21–23, 25
  success of, 26, 27
  work ethic, 125–126
The Scottish Pioneers of Upper Canada, 1755-1855 (Campey), 23
Self-employment, 112–113
Selkirk, Lord, 23, 25
Service industry jobs, 113–118
Shafir, Eldar, 28
Shame
  on asking for help, 18
  food banks and, 95, 96, 97
  isolation and, 32
  social exiles and, 123
Shelter, homeless, 18, 85, 91–93
  See also Food bank; Poverty; Social exile
Simcoe, John Graves, 65

Skills mismatch, 116
Skills training, 114–115
Smith, Barbara. *See* Gilchrist, Barbara
Smith, Mary, 48
Smith, Mary Warner, 48
Smith, Rebecca, 48
Smith, Sarah, 48
Smith, Thomas, 48, 50
Smith, William, 48
Snobbery, food, 99
Social exile
  colonists, 20–25
  home children, 62–63
  homelessness and, 76–80, 92–93
  isolation and, 31–32
  night in coffee shop, 32–35
  trauma and, 72, 80–83
  See also Poverty
Social Housing in Action (SHIA), 92
Socio-economic Inequalities in Suicide Mortality in Quebec, Canada, 1990-2005, 32
Spikes (anti-homeless), 31, 76
Squatters, Dalhousie, 88
Starvation, effects on health, 27
State of Homelessness in Canada, 121
Stereotypes, social exiles, 79–80
Stress, genetics and, 26–27
Suicide, 32
"A Survey of Employment Standard Violations," 114
Sustainable Food Edmonton, 98
Sweden, 85

Talbot, Peter, 53, 125
Talbot, Sophia, 125
Talbot, Wilfred, 53, 125
Tax assessments, 105, 106
Taxation
  credits, 109
  health care premiums as, 105–106

poor taxes, 65, 66, 67, 74
property, 29, 64
See also Guaranteed annual income
TD Bank, 116
Temporary foreign workers, 115–118
The Stop Community Food Centre, 97–98
Thirteen colonies, 23
Toronto
   Great War Veteran's Association, 64
   House of Industry, 57, 60, 66–67
   Regent Park, 91
   urban agriculture, 98
Toronto Evening Star, 67–68
Toronto Globe, 68
Tough Love, 83
Trade-offs
   medications, 44, 103–104
   transportation, 45
Trauma, 26–27, 80–83
Turner, Alina, 79

Underemployment, 109, 111–112, 114–115
Undeserving poor, 67–69, 91, 133, 139
Unemployment
   Canadian Labour Congress on, 111–112
   soldiers and, 23–24, 87
   temporary foreign workers, 116–117
   western migration in 19th Century, 64
United Empire Loyalists (UE), 23
United States
   free market ideology, 74
   jailing the poor, 108
   low wage earners, 111
University of Lethbridge, 27, 82, 117
University of Montreal, 32
Urban agriculture, 98
Urban Housing Task Force, 93

Veterans, 122–123

Waegemakers Schiff, Jeanette, 79
Wages
   foreign workers and, 115–118
   home children, 62
   low, 96, 111–113
Walmart, 113–114
Waste, food, 99
Weadick, Greg, 132
Wellington County
   Garafraxa District, 24
   Home of the Aged, 57
   House of Refuge and Industry, 10, 56–57, 69
   Museum and Archives, 57
Western migration, 64, 75
Widow
   Barbara Gilchrist, 9–10, 49–50
   economic survival, 48, 53, 68
Winnipeg, 71–72
Woolner, Abraham, 24
Woolner, Isaac, 24
Woolner, Jacob, 24
Woolner, Sarah, 24
Woolner, Sarah Gilchrist. See Gilchrist, Sarah
Workers' Action Centre, 114
Workers' Compensation, 74
Working Income Benefit (WITB), 109
Working poor, 11, 89, 93, 96, 103–104, 111–113
Writers' Trust of Canada, 135

York University, 121
Youth
   in crisis, 34–35
   homeless, 93
   See also Children